# The Life Cycle Hypothesis

# The Life Cycle Hypothesis

Groundbreaking new research into the *regular rhythms* and *recurring patterns* that underpin *financial markets*, the *economy* and *human life*

## By Tony Plummer

Hh Harriman House

HARRIMAN HOUSE LTD
18 College Street
Petersfield
Hampshire
GU31 4AD
GREAT BRITAIN
Tel: +44 (0)1730 233870
Email: enquiries@harriman-house.com
Website: www.harriman-house.com

First published in Great Britain in 2018
Copyright © Tony Plummer

The right of Tony Plummer to be identified as the author has been asserted in accordance
with the Copyright, Design and Patents Act 1988.

Paperback ISBN: 978-0-85719-633-0
eBook ISBN: 978-0-85719-634-7

British Library Cataloguing in Publication Data
A CIP catalogue record for this book can be obtained from the British Library.

For the global community of independently-minded technical analysts and economists.

Every owner of a physical copy of this edition of

**The Life Cycle Hypothesis**

can download the eBook for free direct from us at Harriman House, in a format that can be read on any eReader, tablet or smartphone.

Simply head to:

**ebooks.harriman-house.com/lifecyclehypothesis**

to get your free eBook now.

# Contents

# About the author

Tony Plummer has worked and traded in financial markets for more than 40 years. He now specialises in long-term economic and financial research and analysis, and writes and lectures on group behaviour.

Tony is the author of *Forecasting Financial Markets*, which describes the influence of crowd psychology on economic activity and financial market price behaviour. He is also the author of *The Law of Vibration*, which reveals the rhythms, patterns, and levels of support and resistance that were associated with the renowned stock market trader William Gann.

Tony is a former director of Helmsman Economics Ltd, of Rhombus Research Ltd, of Hambros Bank Ltd, and of Hambros Fund Management PLC. He is a Fellow of the Society of Technical Analysts in the UK and was, until November 2011, a Visiting Professorial Fellow in the Department of Economics at Queen Mary, University of London.

He has a Masters degree in economics from the London School of Economics, and an Honours degree in economics from the University of Kent. He has had four years of training in Core Process Psychotherapy.

# Acknowledgements

My thanks go to three groups of people who have made a difference. The first consists of my ex-colleagues at Hambros Bank Ltd, especially David Tapper and John Heywood, who were prepared actively to debate alternative views. The second is formed by the members of the Society of Technical Analysts, especially Deborah Owen, Adam Sorab, Axel Rudolph and Anne Whitby, who encouraged pursuit of the idea that there was a theoretical justification for the regular rhythms and recurring patterns in financial markets. The third group relates to my more recent business career, where regular meetings with high calibre people facilitated a creative interchange of ideas. I am thinking of Robin Aspinall, Robert Brooke, and Peter Warburton, and of clients of Rhombus Research Ltd and Helmsman Economics Ltd who cannot be named.

My thanks, too, have to go to two individuals who are no longer with us, but who book-ended my thought processes between 1980 and 2011: Arthur Koestler and William Gann. Mr Koestler championed the idea that each person has a tendency both to be an individual and to belong to a crowd. Mr Gann's work then made clear that crowd behaviour is characterised by specific rhythms and patterns. His hidden knowledge is the basis of the insights that drove *The Law of Vibration* and, now, *The Life Cycle Hypothesis*. We all stand on the shoulders of the giants who went before us.

And, finally, I must add that none of this would have been possible without the indefatigable support of my partner for this life journey – my wife, Glenys.

# Preface

Life is vibration. Somehow we know this, but we have a tendency to treat the end result as being only quantitative, in order that we might measure it. Yet each vibration has a certain quality to it that enables it to resonate with, harmonise with, and ultimately integrate with, other vibrations.

Out of these qualitative dimensions arises a natural hierarchy. Each part – each vibration – contributes to a greater whole, but that whole is so much greater than just the sum of its parts. Moreover, each element in the hierarchy – including the hierarchy itself – oscillates.

I stretched towards a fuller understanding of this fundamental idea in the various editions of *Forecasting Financial Markets*.[1] My observation was that the interconnected ideas of vibration and hierarchy were almost always ignored in the development of economic theory, and that the resulting policy decisions were ultimately inappropriate.[2]

One of the difficulties facing policy-makers is that vibration incorporates downswings as well as upswings. Indeed, without downswings there could be no upswings, because living systems need periods of rest in order to generate the energy for periods of activity. This means that economic recessions and equity market bear phases cannot be avoided. This is important because evolution is literally transmitted through cyclical patterns. Once economic and financial systems have learnt that there are permanent changes in their environment, a series of fluctuations necessarily emerges. So there are two forces – oscillation and learning – that contribute to the process of change. But this is not all. The third insight – which is now developed more fully in this book – is that the effects of collective learning have a defined life span, and that the associated evolution traverses a very specific pattern. It is this pattern that dominates all economic and social behaviour.

---

[1]   Tony Plummer, *Forecasting Financial Markets* (Kogan Page, London, 1989–2010).
[2]   It is worth mentioning that, after the 2007–09 global financial crisis, the life cycle pattern that is the subject of this book persistently – and correctly – predicted a deflationary environment.

The archetypal pattern is not of my own making. I came very close to defining it in *Forecasting Financial Markets*. So close, in fact, that the correct version of the pattern is almost indistinguishable from the one that I had deduced from the data. This made it particularly easy to recognise the correct configuration when I found it elsewhere. The pattern was hidden in the structure of a book authored by the legendary stock market trader, William Delbert Gann: *The Tunnel Thru The Air*, published in 1927. The pattern turned out also to be present in Mr Gann's esoteric book, *The Magic Word*, published in 1950. The details of my findings were presented in *The Law of Vibration: The Revelation of William D. Gann*, published by Harriman House in early 2013.

In that book, I drew attention to the fact that the pattern had a history. The same basic configuration was hidden in the structure of George I. Gurdjieff's book, *All and Everything: Beelzebub's Tales to his Grandson*, published in 1950. Moreover – and as a sign of its perceived importance – a number of Mr Gurdjieff's students subsequently incorporated a version of the pattern into the physical structure of their own written works. Most amazingly, however, a pattern that is almost identical to Mr Gurdjieff's can be found in the Greek text of St. Matthew's *Gospel* in the Christian *New Testament*. If we assume that the writer(s) of Matthew's *Gospel* lived and worked in a milieu that was already rich in esoteric understandings, then the pattern's ancestry is likely to be very much older than 2,000 years.

According to this lineage, the pattern is timeless, and describes the transmission of energy and information around living systems. Even in its simplest form, the implication is that a living organism either evolves in a precisely configured way after its own creation, or that it responds to the receipt of new information along a predictable trajectory once that evolution has started. In the more complex form that was hidden by Mr Gann, these ideas can now be taken to a whole new level of understanding. They suggest that every living organism is subject to the pressures of a very precisely-defined life cycle. This is the **Life Cycle Hypothesis**.

The idea of a universally applicable life cycle emphatically contradicts the central tenet of postmodern philosophy – that conscious human beings are detached from a cold and meaningless universe.[3] The Life Cycle Hypothesis

---

[3]  The assumption is that awareness itself somehow emerges from the complex interactions of otherwise inert matter. Not only are there serious problems with the logic of this interpretation, but what if the reverse was true? What if matter instead reflects the prior existence of an unknown form of awareness? It is relevant that 80% of the material universe consists of dark (i.e., invisible) matter, and that more than 95% of human DNA is non-coding (i.e., has no obvious function). Taken individually, these absences indicate how little we know; taken together, they suggest that there is a vast quantum field of currently inaccessible energy that is somehow interacting with us. Some scientists are now arguing that this quantum field may have a primordial form of awareness. See, e.g., Ervin Laszlo,

reveals that there are ordered processes behind change, and that the effects of these processes can be tracked over long periods of time and in a variety of contexts. In other words, change and evolution are not independent of some form of deep-structure memory that binds the overall process together. So, for human beings, differentiation does not mean dissociation,[4] short-term variability does not mean long-term randomness, and an inability directly to perceive the relevant organising forces does not mean that those forces do not exist. The universe may, in fact, have purposes beyond the confines of our own limited perceptions.

*The Life Cycle Hypothesis* therefore takes the findings contained in *The Law of Vibration* and extends them into a variety of domains. In the coming chapters, it validates the reality of a time-limited behavioural pattern, shows how this pattern can be used to interpret current financial and economic developments, and explains how the pattern can be used to anticipate future trends. In particular, a careful analysis of the central pattern shows exactly when and where a crisis may be expected to occur. The inference is that such crises are much more deterministic than standard economic theory allows.

## Executive summary

Chapter 1 describes the pattern that was hidden in Mr Gann's *Tunnel Thru The Air*. Chapter 2 outlines the forces that underscore this pattern, and demonstrates the fundamental oscillation in energy as it flows through a living system.

Chapter 3 then presents details of the Life Cycle Hypothesis itself. It shows how unexpected information from the environment generates a new dependent system with an observable life cycle; how that life cycle has two halves, each of which is ended by an energy gap; and how the first of these energy gaps reorientates the system and reconciles external decline with internal development.

Chapter 4 demonstrates the intrinsic importance of the Life Cycle Hypothesis by applying it to the average life span of an individual. This establishes the veracity of William Gann's pattern, and reveals the critical role of the 'mid-life crisis' and the evolutionary function of the second half of life. Chapter 5 extends the ideas into the realm of collective behaviour. It shows how cyclical oscillations differ from each other, and how they can therefore be used to identify the position of a financial market or economy in its greater context.

*Science and the Reenchantment of the Cosmos* (Inner Traditions, Rochester (Vt.), 2006).

4    See Ken Wilber, *Integral Psychology* (Shambhala Publications, Boston (Ma.), 2000).

Chapters 6, 7, and 8 address the forces that have been driving the Dow Jones Industrial Average: Chapter 6 shows the influence of the life cycle between 1907 and 1974; Chapter 7 reveals the influence of the current life cycle; and Chapter 8 explains the fact of a shift into a highly speculative environment at the end of a bull advance.

Chapters 9 and 10 take the analysis into the realm of US industrial production. Chapter 9 looks at the presence of a 36-year cycle in US production data, and shows how the fluctuations within this cycle reveal a great deal about current evolutionary developments. Chapter 10 turns its attention to the influence on economic policy of the Great Depression. It is apparent that a natural slowdown was turned into an outright depression by a failure of understanding. Official attempts to rectify this failure have almost certainly contributed to the problems of inflation after 1973–74, and of deflation after 2008–09.

Chapter 11 reveals that prices of 10-year Treasury Notes in the US have not yet fallen into the energy gap that will generate a long-term signal. Chapter 12 suggests that this is consistent with the evolution of the 54-year Kondratyev Price Cycle. Nevertheless, a major deterioration in inflation expectations still lies ahead.

Chapter 13 shows that recent fluctuations in the euro have been dictated by the currency's need to break with the past. However, it has now embarked on a period in which its status will be transformed.

Chapter 14 explains how shifts in the nature of new product innovation have caused weakness in economic growth. The innovation life cycle that began in the late 18th century may reach the end of its advance just as the Kondratyev Price Cycle reaches its peak.

Finally, Chapter 15 draws together the implications of the Life Cycle Hypothesis for the US, in terms of industrial production, wholesale prices, and T-Note prices. The system seems likely to undergo a major convulsion shortly after 2020.

Tony Plummer
Saffron Walden, 2017

# *1*

# William Gann's Hidden Pattern

## Introduction

IN THE EARLY years of the 2010s decade, I discovered that the legendary stock market trader, William Delbert Gann, had concealed a pattern within the first edition of his famous 1927 book, *The Tunnel Thru The Air* (hereafter *Tunnel*).[5] The full details of how I found the pattern, and deduced its historical lineage, are contained in my 2013 book, *The Law of Vibration*.[6] Those details will not, therefore, be presented here.

The essential point is that Mr Gann concealed the pattern instead of simply revealing it. The book hides a great deal of other information, not the least of which concerns the influence on financial markets of the golden ratio, 38.2:61.8, of the musical octave ratio, 50:100, and of planetary cycles. I shall address the role of the golden ratio and the influence of the musical octave ratio in Appendix II. I shall not, however, be venturing too deeply into the fields of astrology and astronomy.[7] I shall briefly address the role of planetary cycles in Chapter 4, in the context of the human life cycle; otherwise, my intention is to leave the subject to those who know what they're talking about.[8]

---

5    William D. Gann, *The Tunnel Thru The Air* (Financial Guardian Publishing, New York, 1927).
6    Tony Plummer, *The Law of Vibration: The Revelation of William D. Gann* (Harriman House, Petersfield, UK, 2013).
7    It is worth noting that the pattern revealed in *The Law of Vibration* was subsequently found to have a link with astrological constructs. See Olga Morales, *Dawn of the 7th Day*, which can be found at: www.astrologyforganntraders.com.au/-new-book-.html. My working assumption is that symbols of great truths – of which Mr Gann's pattern is one – will necessarily be valid across a variety of arenas.
8    The influence on human behaviour of a deep-running cosmic order is provided, for example, by the distinguished philosopher and cultural historian Richard Tarnas. See Richard Tarnas, *Cosmos and Psyche* (Plume, New York, 2007). It is difficult to recommend a

Meanwhile, we need to know what Mr Gann's pattern actually looks like, so that we can analyse its behavioural implications.

## The pattern

The first edition of *Tunnel* consists of 418 pages, and spans 36 chapters.[9] As a piece of literature it is (for this reader, anyway) tediously long and not particularly engaging. It is full of seemingly irrelevant poems and inappropriate quotations – especially from the *Bible*. This, however, turns out to be a clue, because variations in the text are used as a method of controlling the number of pages in any given chapter. The number of pages per chapter varies significantly, from a low of four to a high of 30. Within the context of the story itself, there is often no obvious reason for variations.

Figure 1-1 plots the number of pages in each chapter against the relevant chapter number. The vertical axes, measuring the number of pages per chapter, start at '1' and end at '30'. The horizontal axes, registering the actual chapter numbers, run from '1' to '36'. It is immediately obvious that the relationship between pages and chapters is not random. There is an obvious low in the 18th chapter, which means that it is halfway through the pattern. Each half consists of a three-wave advance followed by a three-wave contraction. And the absolute high is in the 12th chapter,[10] which is one-third of the way through the pattern.

more appropriate text on the relationship between astronomical alignments and archetypal human behaviour.

9     It cannot be emphasised enough that the information held in the physical structure of the book is inevitably lost in reproductions that take no account of the original typesetting.

10     In ancient philosophy, the number 12 was invariably a reference to the Zodiac – the 12 partitions of the circle of heavens.

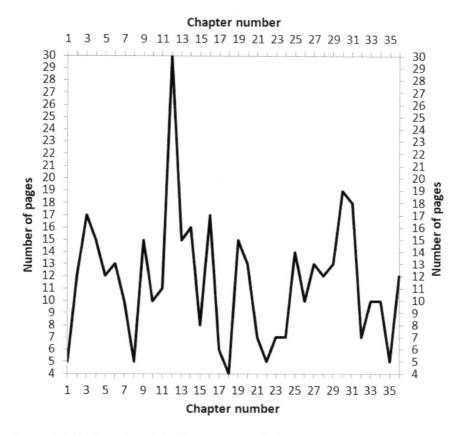

Figure 1-1: William Gann's hidden pattern of vibration

We can tease more information out of this extraordinary pattern by making a series of adjustments to the presentation. First, we can extend the vertical axes so that they run from 0 to 36. This adjustment makes it clear that the pattern can be contained within a square (see Figure 1-2). If we draw a 45-degree line from the bottom left-hand corner of the diagram to the top right-hand corner, the square is complete where 36 pages are equal to 36 chapters – that is, where the book finishes. It is relevant that Mr. Gann used 36 chapters to achieve this effect.

The number 36 is – among other things – almost certainly a reference to the idea of a completed process. If the numerals within the number 36 are separated out into '3' and '6', and then added together, the result is '9' (i.e., 3 + 6 = 9). In esoteric numerology – which Mr Gann persistently used – the number 9 is the number of completion.[11] Coincidentally, the number 36 is also a reference to the 360 degrees of a circle. In this way, Mr Gann was able simultaneously to reference a complete process, a square, and a circle.[12] The use of a 45-degree line means, of course, that the square is also complete where 35 pages are equal to 35 chapters. The rise in the number of pages in the last chapter – Chapter 36 – implies that a new pattern is starting.

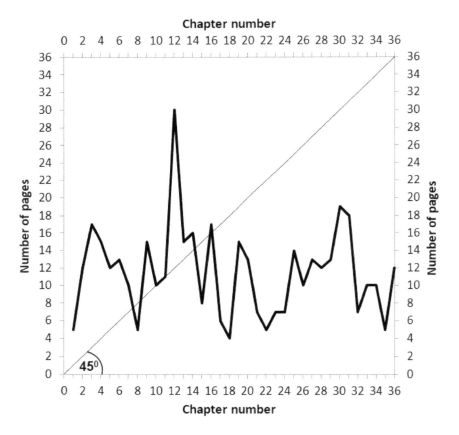

Figure 1-2: The pattern of vibration within a square

---

[11]   The number 9 is central to Mr Gann's esoteric understanding of the universe. It references the enneagram, which is the subject of the next chapter, and it references his Square of Nine. In my opinion, the latter is either an addition to, or an attempt to distract attention from, a diagram called the Circle of Nines. See Appendix I.

[12]   In sacred geometry, the square represents Earth and the circle represents Heaven. We thus have a hint in the diagram of an external manifestation of an internal – and therefore hidden – process. It is also worth noting that the square is identified with the number '4'.

## Initial interpretations

We can now add simple notations to the diagram in order to highlight the relationships between the waves. In the first set of notations, the first (rising) phase of the diagram is denoted 1-2-3; the subsequent (falling) section is marked A-B-C; and the fluctuations within the (rising) wave B are designated a-b-c. See Figure 1-3.

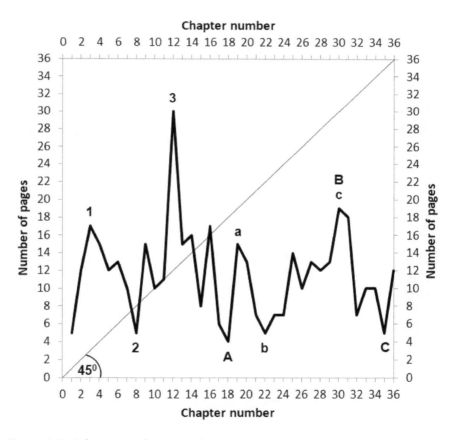

Figure 1-3: Advance and contraction

In this formation, the diagram represents a strong three-wave advance (i.e., 1-2-3), followed by an extended three-wave correction (i.e., A-B-C). Within the correction, the rising wave has three phases (i.e., a-b-c). This emphasises that movements are cyclic in the sense that each advance is followed by a contraction. It also emphasises that the process is ordered because: (a) each movement consists of three waves; and (b) the advancing phase is one-third of the whole cycle, and the contracting phase is two-thirds of that cycle.

The alternative set of notations is shown in Figure 1-4. Here, the diagram is divided into two parts, consisting of 18 chapters each. The major rising waves to the left and right of the centre point are denoted 1-2-3; the sub-waves within those rising waves are denoted i-ii-iii; and each rising wave is followed by a three-phase fall, with the sub-waves denoted A-B-C.

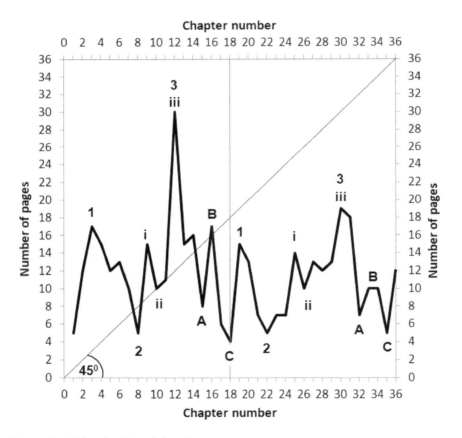

Figure 1-4: The duality of the diagram

In this formulation, the diagram reveals the presence of two very similar oscillations consisting of an extended three-wave advance (1-2-3) followed by a very sharp three-wave contraction (A-B-C). Moreover, each advance-and-contraction takes half of the diagram. If the two halves of the diagram are overlaid on each other, it is possible to make direct comparisons. See Figure 1-5.

In both cases, a base pattern provides the foundation for an impulse wave that takes wave 3 to a new high. In the first half of the diagram, the base pattern is extended and the impulse wave is dramatic. In the second half of the diagram, the base pattern is relatively brief and the subsequent impulse wave is extended. Both patterns are followed by falls that return the locus of movement back to the bottom of the base formation. In the first half of the chart, the locus actually drops to a new low.

The presence of a dual oscillation suggests that the second half of the diagram in some way repeats the processes of the first half. This will prove to be very relevant when we explore the concept of a life cycle.

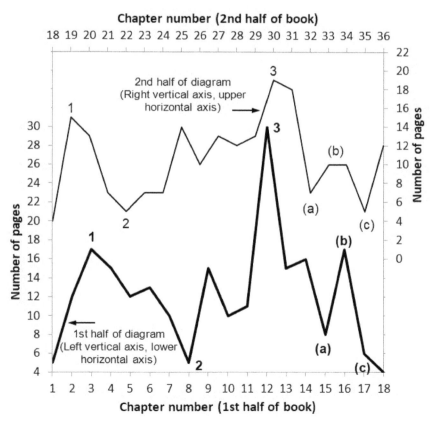

Figure 1-5: Comparing the two halves of the diagram

## Conclusion

There is a pattern embedded in the structure of the first edition of *Tunnel*, which appears to have been very carefully constructed. Even at first sight, it looks non-random. A closer consideration shows it to be based both on the idea of a cycle and on the combined roles of duality (up and down) and of trinity (reconciling force, active force, and passive force) in that cycle. The presence of the pattern in Mr Gann's book is certainly a testimony to his genius; and to go to so much trouble is evidence of a desire to transmit the intrinsic information to others.

In my opinion, the information revealed by Mr Gann incorporates the importance of oscillations in evolution, the three-wave nature of an impulse move, and (implicitly) the fact that an energetic system learns by adapting its internal structure to an information shock. This is the basis of what I am going to call the **Life Cycle Hypothesis**.

The fundamental idea is that new energy, which arrives in the form of a shock, creates a new dynamic structure with an appropriate set of internal processes. The resulting organism may be psychological or physical, but it becomes a living reality with a beginning, a pre-ordered existence, and a definable end. It is in many ways one of the answers to the nihilism of so-called post-modern deconstruction, where all meaning is context-dependent and therefore ambiguous. The Life Cycle Hypothesis points to the presence of an ordered framework behind the process of learning, change, and evolution.

# 2

## The Symbolic Enneagram

### Introduction

It is important to be clear about the concepts that are being introduced. The starting point is that: (a) a living system – which in some sense has a memory – is generated by a creative shock of some kind; and that (b) this new system has a life cycle.

Modern analysis is already familiar with the idea of a process that starts at birth and ends at death.[13] It is less clear, however, about the forces that link the moment of creation with the moment of termination. In addition, although it is easy to extend the basic ideas beyond a single living organism (such as an animal or a human being) to even more complex structures (such as a corporation or a society), it is much less easy to tell when a specific stage of development has been reached. Is a mid-life crisis a real event? How can we tell when a company is transforming itself into a more sustainable organisation? What are the signs of a political party being in its death throes?

The point that has invariably been missed is that the processes of evolution are precise and universal: they apply to a newly created system; they are relevant to sub-systems within an existing system; and they journey through specific stages. Hence, a system, or sub-system, is brought into being by the force of new information, and the subsequent behaviour of that system is ordered, patterned, and (therefore) to a large extent predictable.

---

[13] For completion, I have included a commentary on the conventional 'S'-shaped learning curve in Appendix IV.

## The Law of Three and the Law of Seven

In *The Law of Vibration*, I suggested that the source of Mr Gann's pattern was his knowledge of an ancient diagram known as the enneagram. This diagram was introduced into Western philosophy in the first half of the 20th century by George Ivanovitch Gurdjieff.[14] It describes the way that an initiating information shock generates an oscillating flow of energy within a learning system. The great secret is that the initiating force of new information comes from outside the system itself but is then internalised by a three-up/three-down oscillation.

It is therefore no small matter that, in *Tunnel*, Mr Gann references the enneagram in his use of chapter numbers and titles. Specifically, Chapter XXXIV is denoted Chapter XXXIX. At first glance, this appears to be a mistake, caused by the use of an 'X' rather than a 'V'. But it is not. Nothing in *Tunnel* is accidental. The exchange of Roman numerals is an application of numerology, based on the simple idea of adding the digits of any number together.[15]

The first point is that, had the correct chapter number been used, the numerals would have added to 7 (i.e., 3 + 4). Instead, Mr Gann uses the phrase "Robert Gordon's Seven Days" as a subtitle for the chapter, and thereby maintains a reference to the number 7. The second point is that the digits in the number 'XXXIX' (i.e., '39') initially sum to 12 (i.e., 3 + 9), and then add to 3 (i.e., 1 + 2). In this way, Mr Gann has very cleverly referenced the numbers '7' and '3' in the same context. This is a direct reference to the two cosmic laws that are represented by the enneagram – the Law of Seven and the Law of Three.

## Information shocks and cycles

This is not the place to go into a huge amount of detail about the workings of these two great laws. They are covered in *The Law of Vibration*,[16] and detailed analyses can be found in numerous relevant texts.[17] It is, however, appropriate to give a brief overview of the way in which new information creates a circular process within a living system.

In Figure 2-1, which shows the symbolic version of the enneagram, the external shock enters the circle at the peak of the three-sided triangle. As a result of the

---

[14] See, for example, Kenneth Walker, *A Study of Gurdjieff's Teaching* (Jonathan Cape, London, 1957).

[15] The proper transmission of Mr Gann's knowledge is made impossible in reprints of *Tunnel* that presume to rectify his alleged errors.

[16] Tony Plummer, *The Law of Vibration: The Revelation of William D. Gann* (Harriman House, Petersfield, UK, 2013).

[17] See, for example, Pyotr D. Ouspensky, *In Search Of the Miraculous* (Harcourt, Brace & World, New York, 1949).

shock, the energy oscillation starts at '1', drops to '4', and then rises to '2'. In theory, this move is controlled by an internally-generated push upwards from point '3'. This latter represents the active aspect of the process. The power of this impulse then enables the energy flow to traverse the circle to point '8'. The result is a three-wave movement.

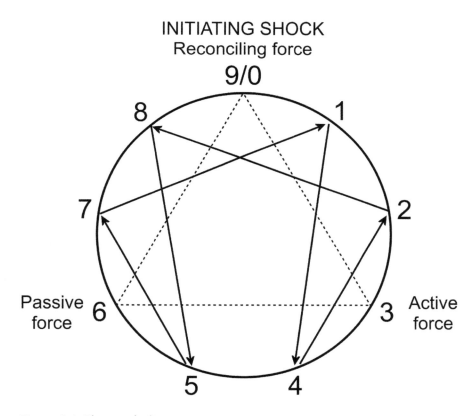

Figure 2-1: The symbolic enneagram

In the absence of a new input of energy at the top of the triangle – i.e., at point '9' – the system necessarily reverses direction by dropping to point '5'. This is the beginning of a downswing. The system first recovers to point '7', but an internally-generated pull at point '6' drags the system downwards. This corresponds to the passive (or rest) energy within the process, and the system accordingly shifts (i.e., drops) to point '1'. Again, the result is a three-wave movement.

In this way, the enneagram has generated a cycle. The energy shock at the top of the triangle plus the resulting six-wave oscillation represents a seven-part movement. This is the Law of Seven. Moreover, the oscillation is controlled by the triangle. Since this triangle controls the oscillation, it remains hidden. The upper corner of the triangle (i.e., '9' or '0') has a dual function: it provides the stimulative shock, and it indicates the presence of a governing force that controls (or reconciles) the balance between the active and passive energies in the subsequent process. The other two corners of the triangle ('3' and '6') represent those two energies – respectively the active force and the passive force – as the system responds to the shock. This is the Law of Three.

## The enneagram pulse

The resulting cycle is shown graphically in Figure 2-2. The vertical axis represents the movement through the six numbers 1, 2, 4, 5, 7, and 8. These are the enneagram's 'nodes'. The horizontal axis, on the other hand, represents the passage of time. In this model, there are seven units of time, numbered from 1 to 7.

The process starts with a creative shock that is generated from outside the system being analysed. This shock – i.e., the change that makes a change[18] – arrives at point '0'. Then, provided that there is not a subsequent stimulus at reversal node '9',[19] an oscillation materialises. This oscillation takes the form of a three-up/three-down movement – i.e., 1-2-3 for the rising phase and A-B-C for the falling phase.

As we shall see, this pattern incorporates a learning process. In the meantime, we can note that phase 2 and phase B are contra-trend movements; that the phase 2 drop back to the original low is functionally related to the active force of the enneagram (reversal node 3); and that the phase B recovery back to the high is controlled by the passive force (reversal node 6). In other words, neither the phase 2 drop nor the phase B recovery reflects just the withdrawal of energy

---

[18]   The idea that information was "a change that makes a change" was championed by Gregory Bateson in *Mind and Matter – An Essential Unity* (Wildwood House, London, 1979).

[19]   It is not my intention to analyse the consequences of an input of new energy at reversal node 9. It is sufficient to state that: (a) a new three up/three down pattern becomes concatenated onto the original oscillation; (b) the rising phase transmutes into an extended five-wave pattern; and (c) the original A-B-C downwave disappears. This is one explanation of the 5-3 pattern that underlies the Elliott Wave Principle. The classic work on this formation is Robert R. Prechter and Alfred J. Frost's *The Elliott Wave Principle* (New Classics Library, New York, 1978).

from the overarching trend. The retracements involve a form of covert activity even while the overt energy pattern is materialising.

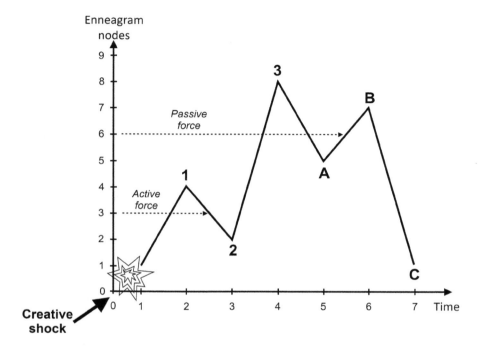

Figure 2-2: The enneagram pulse

## The third force

For Figure 2-2 to be valid, the cycle formation must be contained within, and be subject to, some form of **holding field**. Moreover, because of the nature of life, this holding field must necessarily be part of a hierarchy. For example, electrons chunk-up into atoms, atoms group into molecules, molecules collect into organ systems, and organ systems assemble into living organisms. Each unit in the hierarchy has both a tendency to be itself and a tendency to belong to a higher grouping.[20]

But conventional theory tends to see this natural structuring as having a limit: the hierarchy bifurcates into human and non-human, and then it stops for

20   Arthur Koestler, *Janus: A Summing Up* (Hutchinson, London, 1978).

humans. It is assumed that the neocortex of the human brain, which provides the ability to think rationally, detaches humankind from the natural forces that influence the animal world. Consequently, human beings will not (except perhaps very loosely and/or in very unusual circumstances) collect into higher groupings, even though animals can chunk-up into herds. And, of course, no account is taken of the possibility that all living creatures are part of a greater whole.

In Mr Gurdjieff's terminology, the hierarchy of holding fields represents the influence of the 'third force', without which no living system can exist.[21] This force is the one that guides the energy flows through a living system. It will also therefore insert the influences of the active and passive forces where appropriate. This means that the third force must have access to a memory of some sort, so that it knows what has come before the current moment; and it must be able to organise oscillations, so that it can direct future behaviour.

In *The Law of Vibration*, I observed that these processes involved the application of **learning**,[22] and therefore the transfer of short-term experience into longer-term memory. Before addressing this process directly, it can be noted that, without a holding field and its associated learning, there would be genuine chaos. Any movement of energy would result in a non-predictable follow-through. Under these circumstances, a 'system' simply could not exist. However, with a holding field that persists through time, the pattern shown in Figure 2-2 becomes perfectly feasible. The holding field is, in a sense, stable.

## The learning pattern

The presence of a holding field is part of the natural structure that allows a living system to respond to the changes in its environment. The changes themselves impact as an energy shock, and the response from a living system involves learning that a change has occurred.[23] The important point is that this learning has a very specific three-phase profile: (a) an initial reaction that does not involve an alteration in the system's parameters; (b) the alteration of the system's internal structure to accommodate the new information; and (c) a full response by the system to the changed conditions.

It is the second stage of this process that causes difficulty because the outward signs do not necessarily reflect the inner adjustments. Usually, the external (and therefore measurable) behavioural indicators will undergo a reversal. This, though, hides the fact that the system has become stressed by the changes in

---

[21]   Pyotr D. Ouspensky, *op cit.*
[22]   Tony Plummer, *op cit.*
[23]   Learning is not restricted to the mental assimilation of knowledge.

its environment, and is altering its inner structure in order to cope. In other words, stress triggers learning.

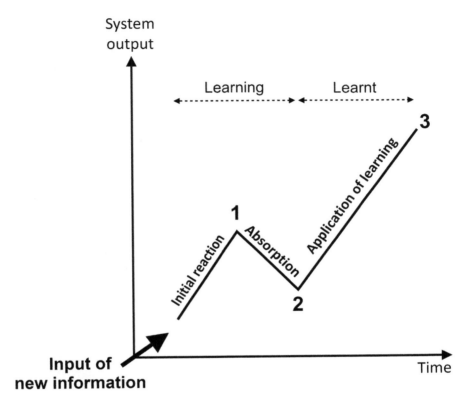

Figure 2-3: The learning pattern

On this analysis, the second phase of a learning process involves a retracement – either in whole or in part – of the first phase.[24] This is shown in Figure 2-3, where the vertical axis represents the system's output (whatever that may be) and the horizontal axis shows the passage of time. A change in the environment impacts on the system as an input of new energy; the system reacts to that change (phase 1), but then retraces part or all of that reaction (phase 2). Once the implications of the change have been absorbed, system output can expand on the basis of a transformed inner structure (phase 3). Hence, phases 1 and 2

---

24    The presence of this retracement is itself evidence of some form of intelligence.

represent the learning phase of the pattern,[25] while phase 3 is the application of that learning.

## Energy gaps

One of the important features of the three-phase learning process is that it is driven by the arrival of new information. There are, in fact, two types of stimulus in the symbolic enneagram: the first is the originating shock; the second is system overload. The two phenomena are very different, and so need to be properly distinguished from each other.

Theoretically, the original information shock will set the system moving. Initially, of course, the organism has to accept, or learn, that the environment has changed irreversibly. Once this learning has taken place, the system will move to the limits of its capacity. This then generates the second type of information, which is that the system cannot progress any further. The system therefore falls into an **energy gap**. Such a gap represents the onset of a rest phase, without which the system's energies cannot be restored. Theoretically, the gap occurs after reversal node 8 and before reversal node 1 in Figure 2-1 and Figure 2-2.[26] It is not just a mirror image of the originating shock, and so cannot bring with it the forces that will stop the cycle from turning down. Indeed, the downturn in the cycle represents the **absence** of a new shock.[27]

In practical terms, this means that the energy gap in a living system corresponds to the phase A drop in Figure 2-2. It will therefore arise when the phase 3 upswing has gone as far as it can. In other words, the energy gap will impact when the active processes of the system are exhausted. The next stage, of course, is that the system has to absorb the implications. Is the exhaustion temporary? Or is it more permanent? The system therefore goes through a learning stage, which is phase B in Figure 2-2. Eventually, when the learning is complete, the final stage of the downswing materialises. This is the period when the internal processes reassign energy to exhausted elements of the system and release unneeded resources back to the environment. It corresponds to phase C in Figure 2-2.

---

[25]   A setback during the process of learning has long been recognised. Henry Mills reported evidence of students needing time to digest that which has been taken in during training (*Teaching and Training*, Macmillan, 1967). Donald Hebb saw it as involving the transfer of information from short-term to long-term memory (*The Organisation of Behaviour*, John Wiley, New York, 1949).

[26]   See Tony Plummer, *op cit*.

[27]   This is the basic point that is missed by policy-makers in the field of economic activity.

# Continuous oscillations

It follows, of course, that once the phase C downswing has gone as far as it can, then the restoration processes within the passive phase of the cycle will be complete. Consequently, the rest phase of the process will have reached a natural limit, and conditions will be consistent with the return of the active phase. Consequently, a phase 1 upswing will begin. It is important, therefore, to note what has happened. An initiating shock triggers a cycle that will persist. Figure 2-4 shows that a 1-2-3 upswing is followed by an A-B-C downswing; that this downswing is then followed by another 1-2-3 upswing; and so on. Within this recurring cycle, each phase 2 and each phase B represent the absorption of information, while the turning points at the end of each phase 3 and each phase C are caused by satiation.

If we look at the enneagram in Figure 2-1, it can be seen that both types of turning point occur at the top of the enneagram, between node 8 and node 1. Both are caused by satiation, but one type is caused by the exhaustion of the active phase (this is the **energy gap**), while the other emerges at the end of the passive phase (and is best classified as an **energy stimulus**). This is the basis of a persistent rhythm. There is, of course, the question of how long the oscillations can continue, which we shall deal with in due course. The answer depends on the life cycle of the system that has been set in process by the initiating shock.

Figure 2-4: The enneagram pulse

## Conclusion

The symbolic enneagram is a teaching tool. It provides a profound insight into the fundamental forces that generate oscillations in a living system. It reveals that cycles are natural, that a passive phase is necessary to restore the energy that is lost during an active phase, and that there will be a continuous fluctuation between active and passive phases driven by specific stimuli.

These stimuli differ from each other in the sense that one represents the exhaustion of an active phase of the cycle, while the other is caused by the revitalisation of the system during the passive phase of its cycle. The former is an energy gap, while the latter is an energy stimulus. In both cases, the shifts in energy are a function of a reconciling (or third) force. Such a force is, however, not universally recognised by conventional analysis.

# 3

## The Life Cycle Hypothesis

### Introduction

THE VERSION OF the enneagram explored in Chapter 2 is only **symbolic**. It is the version that was taught by the mindfulness exponent, George Gurdjieff, in the first half of the 20th century.[28] This teaching diagram demonstrates the energetic forces behind a cyclical rise and fall in a system, but it does not necessarily reflect either the complete pattern or the total life cycle of the system being considered. It is therefore significant that Mr Gurdjieff hid another version of the enneagram in the physical structure of his own work, *All and Everything*.[29] Moreover, this version was very similar to the one hidden in *Tunnel* by Mr Gann, and which was reproduced in Chapter 1.[30]

I have covered elsewhere the parallels between the Gurdjieff and Gann patterns, and the similarities of both with the pattern hidden in the Greek version of St. Matthew's *Gospel* in the *New Testament*.[31] The important point is that, although the hidden Gurdjieff/Gann pattern exhibits the primary three-up (i.e., 1-2-3) and three-down (i.e., A-B-C) configuration that is typical of the symbolic enneagram, there are at least three additional developments. Specifically, the peak of the hidden cycle occurs in the first half of the pattern, rather than in the middle; its recovery in the second half of the pattern is long and slow; and this second-half recovery consists of three very clear phases. Mr Gurdjieff and Mr Gann were obviously aware of the presence of other influences.

---

28 Details are contained in, for example, Pyotr D. Ouspensky, *In Search of the Miraculous* (Harcourt, Brace & World, New York, 1949).
29 George I. Gurdjieff, *All and Everything* (Routledge & Kegan Paul, London, 1950).
30 William D. Gann, *The Tunnel Thru The Air* (Financial Guardian Publishing, New York, 1927).
31 Tony Plummer, *The Law of Vibration* (Harriman House, Petersfield, UK, 2013).

# Mr Gurdjieff and Mr Gann

Although the historical evidence suggests that Mr Gurdjieff was the primary source of the teaching enneagram, the great paradox is that his book containing the secret version was published almost a quarter of a century after Mr Gann's book.[32] This allows at least three possibilities: first, both men were drawing from a common source; second, Mr Gann's early work on vibration was incomplete until he was made aware in the 1920s (but well before *All and Everything* was published) of Mr Gurdjieff's teachings;[33] or, third, Mr Gurdjieff found out about Mr Gann's method of hiding an advanced version of the enneagram and decided to use the same method in his own book. Whatever the truth, Mr Gann probably still felt obliged to hide the essential pattern because he knew – at that time – it was supposed not to be widely disseminated.[34]

The fact that the pattern was different to the teaching diagram, and was in some sense secret, takes us a step closer to being able to understand the depths of the message that was being transmitted. Firstly, the similarity between Mr Gurdjieff's pattern and that of Mr Gann means that both men knew that an enhanced version existed. Secondly, the significant body of written work that surrounds Mr Gurdjieff's ideas means that we have access to the logic behind the enneagram. And thirdly, since this logic relates to change and evolution in living systems, we can apply the ideas to humankind.

The implications are extraordinary. One of these is that, if the Gurdjieff/Gann enneagram pattern can be applied to collective behaviour in financial markets or economies, then we have strong grounds for supposing that the conventional methods of analysing such behaviour are incomplete, or even incorrect. And if this is the case, then it can only be concluded that we are approaching a major paradigm shift.

# A self-organising system

The Gurdjieff/Gann pattern unfolds in response to a creative shock. Such a shock is a unique item of information that arrives at a specific moment in time. It is, to use Gregory Bateson's terminology, "a difference that makes a difference".[35] But the fact that information triggers a distinctive pattern says

---

[32]   Mr Gurdjieff's book (*All and Everything*) was published in 1950, whereas Mr Gann's work (*The Tunnel Thru The Air*) was published in 1927. However, Mr Gurdjieff's ideas were already circulating in the US in the 1920s.

[33]   The information may have come either directly from Mr Gurdjieff, or from one of the teachers appointed by Mr Gurdjieff.

[34]   It is said that Mr Gann was in conflict with his Methodist family over his beliefs.

[35]   Gregory Bateson, *Mind and Matter – An Essential Unity* (Wildwood House, London,

something about the system. It suggests that the system has the ability to organise itself.

A **self-organising system** has certain specific characteristics: interacting components; interactions triggered by differences; access to energy to drive the interactions; the use of feedback loops; and an immanent ability to be something greater than the sum of its parts. Gregory Bateson considered that any system that demonstrated this matrix of qualities could also be considered to be a living system. Moreover, such systems evolve in response to creative shocks. It is therefore no small matter that financial markets and economies can be viewed as self-organising systems.[36]

## The creative shock

A creative shock can take many forms. On the positive side, it could entail the fertilisation of an egg within a womb; it might include the introduction of a new product in an economy; it could be a new idea in relation to an existing body of theory; or it could even involve an expansion of consciousness within a human body. On the negative side, the information shock may be the intrusion of a virus into another organism; it might be an act of aggression by one or more people within a socio-political milieu; or it might be the emergence of a leader who can propel a psychological crowd to upset an existing set of social conditions. The list is endless.

Sometimes, of course, the shock may not be obvious either at the time or until long after the event. The basic point, however, is that differences between a system and its environment will eventually trigger a response. The new idea relating to the Gurdjieff/Gann pattern is that this response may necessitate the evolution either of the system itself or of a new system within the old system. In either sense, the evolving system is a new phenomenon.

## The consequences

There are two aspects to this idea. Firstly, there is the emergence of the new self-organising system. This new system will have a starting point (i.e., 'birth') and a finishing point (i.e., 'death'). Secondly, the new system will inhabit a **holding field**. It will not just exist in a vacuum. The relationship between the system and the holding field will involve a process of learning. The relationship will be

---

1979). In the arena of collective behaviour, the impact may be preceded by a period that involves the gathering together of ideas, of intentions, and/or of physical innovations. A difference is created between what **is**, and what **could be**. The creative shock then emerges as a distinct phenomenon as an attempt to reduce this difference.

36    Tony Plummer, *Forecasting Financial Markets* (Kogan Page, London, 1989–2010).

two-way and, once it has started, it cannot be stopped except by the premature ending of whatever it is that constitutes the system.

There are then two specific revelations that materialise from the work of Mr Gann and Mr Gurdjieff. The first is that the **consequences** of a creative shock are not random. They proceed on the basis of a pre-given template, or instruction set. This template involves a specific pattern that persists through time, that manages evolutionary development, and that therefore links seemingly random events together. The second revelation follows from this. It is likely that each new system has a **purpose** beyond its own existence.[37] The second half of each evolutionary pattern seems orientated towards the apparent death of the system. Since Nature does not waste energy, there must be an objective that underlies this particular orientation.

The accuracy and power of these ideas should become apparent as the analysis progresses. For the moment, it seems clear that the Gurdjieff/Gann pattern points to the existence of laws within Nature that are not currently recognised by science.

## Mr Gann's pattern

In order to keep the analysis simple, I shall concentrate only on one pattern – that concealed by Mr Gann. His diagram, which was surveyed in Chapter 1, is reproduced as Figure 3-1. The vertical axis represents an energy index of some sort, and the horizontal axis tracks the passage of time. The diagram accordingly represents the flow of energy through a living system. The flow emerges after a creative shock: there is a marked leftwards bias in the timing of the peak; a noticeable low in the middle of the pattern; and a three-phase oscillation in the final rising wave.

As presented, the move into the peak is denominated 1-2-3, and the subsequent move into the final low is denoted A-B-C. This means that the pattern is being treated **as if** it reflected the dynamics of the symbolic enneagram. On this basis, the 1-2-3 segment is the active, growth, phase of the pattern, while the A-B-C segment is the passive, or contracting, phase of the pattern. But there are three major changes. Firstly, the collapse that includes the energy gap (i.e., the A-wave) is very pronounced. Secondly, the subsequent recovery (the B-wave) is extended. And thirdly, each of the major swings consists of three distinct phases.

---

37   Beyond this point, I shall use the terms 'system', 'organism', and 'paradigm' interchangeably. In a functional sense, they are identical to each other.

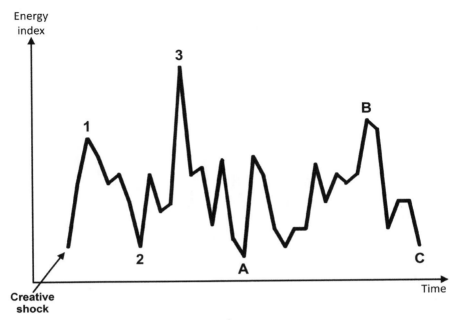

Figure 3-1: Mr Gann's pattern revisited

## The A-wave

It is apparent from Figure 3-1 that the falling A-wave consists of two separate parts, interspersed with a recovery. The most obvious interpretation is that the energy gap initially seems to have finished but that, just when the worst seems to be over, a crisis emerges. This is shown in Figure 3-2. The idea of an energy gap followed by a crisis would also help to explain why the subsequent B-wave takes some time to evolve.

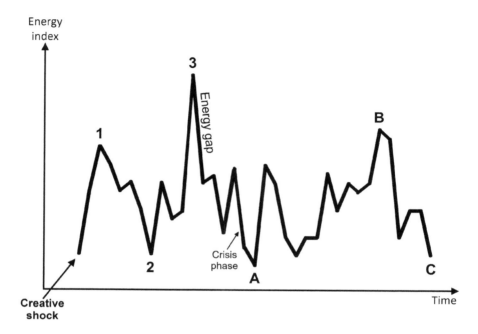

Figure 3-2: Energy gap and crisis

## Two halves and two learning patterns

There is, however, another interpretation of the whole diagram, which was mentioned in Chapter 1. It is quite clear that the pronounced low at point A of Figure 3-1 and Figure 3-2 splits the diagram into two parts. At this point, the first half of the pattern finishes and the second half begins. The whole system has in some way been reorientated.

Importantly, the pattern in the second half of the diagram effectively recapitulates the pattern of the first half. One inference is that the energy fluctuations in the diagram contain **two** learning phases: the first occurs immediately after the creative shock; the second appears after the system has been revitalised. This aspect of the dual nature of the life cycle is shown in Figure 3-3.

The idea of two learning phases during the evolution of a life cycle is important. The first learning phase (i.e., waves 1[1] and 2[1] in Figure 3-3) is **primary** in the sense that it is the initial response to the creative shock. It is the period during which the system recognises that a change has occurred in its holding field and then adjusts itself in order to cope with it. This process is automatic and need not involve conscious awareness.

The second learning phase (i.e., waves $1^2$ and $2^2$ in Figure 3-3) is **adaptive**. It is the internal change that the system has to undergo after being reorientated by the energy gap/crisis at the end of the first half of the cycle. The second learning phase can only take place after the structures of the first half of the whole cycle have been put in place, and after the system has stopped supplying energy for the creation of those structures.

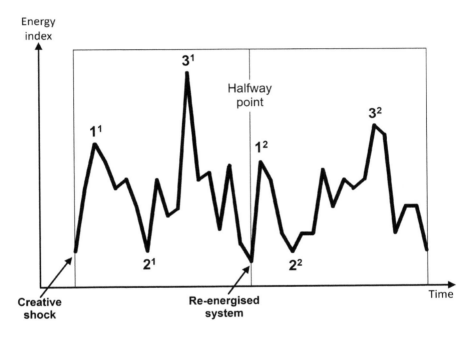

Figure 3-3: System learning

## Duality

This interpretation has a startling effect on the full implications of the diagram. Firstly, it means that the structure that is formed during the first half of the diagram will support activity during the second half, but will lose importance. In most of the circumstances that we are able to observe, the structure will simply die away. This is the 1-2-3/A-B-C version of the diagram.

Secondly, the dual interpretation indicates that the energy gap that materialises at the end of the first half of the pattern will be replicated in some way at the end of the second half. This is the 1-2-3/1-2-3 interpretation. This second energy gap will then, in effect, terminate the whole pattern. These characteristics of the diagram are shown in Figure 3-4.

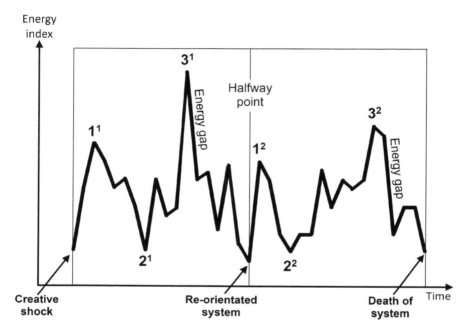

Figure 3-4: System energy gaps

## Reconciliation

If **both** interpretations are applicable, then the energy gap at the end of the second half of the diagram will coincide with the C-wave of Figure 3-1 and Figure 3-2. This suggests that there must be something in the second half of the diagram that undergoes a sustained period of growth, but which nevertheless takes place while the original system is contracting. For simplicity, these two halves can be called, respectively, 'external' and 'internal'. However, the terms may need careful interpretation under different circumstances.

The most likely possibility is that the first half of the pattern builds the supporting structures of the living system, and that the second half of the pattern concentrates on enhancing the internal processes of that system (whatever they may be). This means that the energy gap/crisis at the end of the first half automatically triggers a switch from external growth to internal growth.

The inference therefore is that, while the external structures are contracting and moving the system towards termination (see Figure 3-5), energy is diverted towards internal work (see Figure 3-6). If this is correct, it also strongly suggests that the internal work has a purpose beyond the confines of the system's life span.[38] Why would Nature waste its energy on diverting resources from external structures to internal processes?

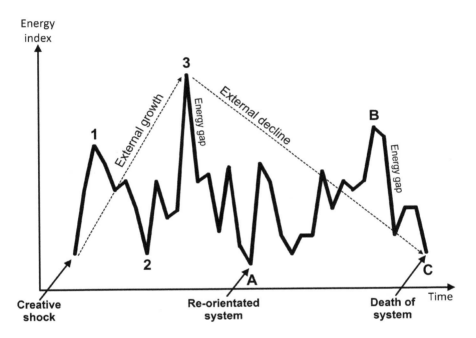

Figure 3-5: External system

[38] A very good example relates to the growth of a foetus within its mother's womb, and then the evolution of the neonate in the outside world. In this case, there is a clear link between the two phases that is reflected in the birth process. The Gann pattern can be applied between conception and the start of the birth process, and then between birth itself and death. But it raises questions about whether the pattern is then applicable after death.

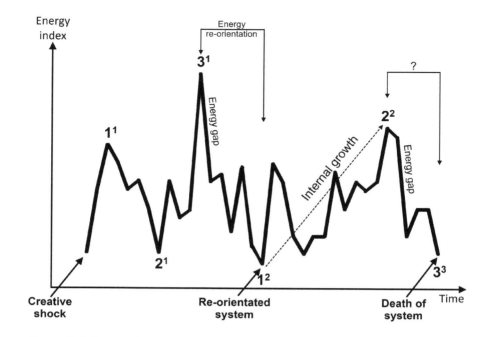

Figure 3-6: Internal system

## Three from two

On this interpretation, the second half of the system's life is triggered by an internalised switch of direction, and incorporates a period of change that builds on the experiences of the first half of the diagram. Neither is likely to be picked up by a casual observer, but both imply the presence of a holding field that in some way is involved with the process. Almost certainly, this is part of the message that William Gann himself was trying to convey in the structure of his 1950 book, *The Magic Word*.[39]

On this analysis, it is possible to view the whole pattern as a reflection of an overarching learning process such as was shown in Figure 2-3. Here, however, the pattern necessarily includes a terminal phase that acknowledges the end (or death) of the learning and/or the learning system. This idea is shown in Figure 3-7. Firstly, the initial energy gap and its aftermath can be reclassified as

---

[39] The pattern suggests that Mr Gann himself believed in the continuation of life after the body had died. William D. Gann, *The Magic Word* (Library of Gann Publishing Co, Pomeroy (Wa.), 1950). See also Tony Plummer, *The Law of Vibration* (Harriman House, Petersfield, UK, 2013).

belonging to the absorption phase of a higher-level learning pattern. Secondly, the learning that is acquired during that absorption phase will be applied during the second half of the pattern. And thirdly, of course, the effects will be cumulative.

The presence of a higher-level – and ongoing – learning process means that the mechanics of the whole system belong to a higher level of meaning. The cycle has two halves – one external and one internal – but it also has an overall dynamic that contains and directs both. This means that the lower order parts contribute to the whole and that the whole is more than just the sum of its parts. A third formation is immanent in – and therefore arises from – the two halves. The pattern is, in effect, that of a **life cycle**.

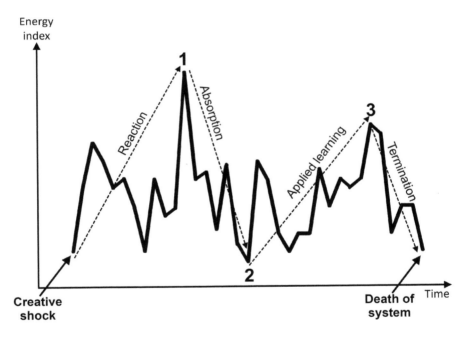

Figure 3-7: Higher-level learning cycle

## Conclusion

The hypothesis being proposed here is that a creative shock will initiate a new system, within a wider holding field. The creative shock is the energetic effect of new information; the resulting system will have a **life cycle**, which runs from birth to death; and the life cycle will ensure that the system has access both to a memory of where it's been and to a pathway into the future. Once the growth of whatever it is that constitutes the new system has started, it cannot be stopped except by the premature death of the system itself.

Under these circumstances, a newly-created system and a living system are functionally identical. This has some remarkable implications if the system involves collective behaviour. Quite apart from anything else it means that such behaviour can be treated as if it is a living organism. It also means that, once a change has been initiated, that change will take a sustained period of time to complete. This introduces the phenomenon of time directly into the process of development. It also therefore provides a link between events that might otherwise seem independent of each other.

These conclusions are completely at odds with the idea of randomness that pervades the social sciences, and they point to the need for a major paradigm shift. The pattern that was hidden by St Matthew in the Christian *New Testament*, by George Gurdjieff in *All and Everything*, and by William Gann in *Tunnel Thru The Air*, could not have more profound implications.

# *4*

# The Human Life Cycle

## Introduction

ONE OF THE conclusions in Chapter 3 is that there is an important difference between the two halves of Mr Gann's life cycle pattern. There seems to be a mechanism that creates a switch in focus from external structures to internal processes. The mechanism involves an energy gap, and a crisis of some sort. This implies that the energy gap and crisis are pre-programmed and that there is a purpose behind the resulting switch. It also means that the mid-life transition is a real phenomenon that applies to everyone. The fact that certain occurrences are not obvious does not mean that they don't exist. This has profound implications for our understanding of personal change and evolution.

## The life cycle pattern for a human being

Since it is likely that Mr Gann was trying to convey a very particular form of knowledge in *Tunnel*, it is possible that he intended it to be used for individual human beings. If so, we need to identify the relationship between the total number of chapters and a human life span.

In fact, that relationship is very simple because we can convert chapter numbers into human ages. The first chapter of *Tunnel* would represent 'birth'; so, it will have to be treated as '0'. The second chapter will then become '1', the third will be '2', and so forth. This shift means that, although the total number of chapters relevant to a life cycle remains unchanged at 35, the 35th chapter will be denoted '34'. The next stage is to divide each of the numbers between 0 and 34 by 35, and multiply the result by 100. Once rounded to the nearest whole number, each of the integers can be taken as an indication of an individual's age. By definition, these ages – and therefore a potential human lifetime – will stretch from 0 to 97.

The relationship between this life span and Mr Gann's pattern is shown in Figure 4-1. The ages themselves are shown both along the top horizontal axis and at each of the major turning points in the diagram. In principle, it should be possible to identify the state of personal evolution for each specific year of life.

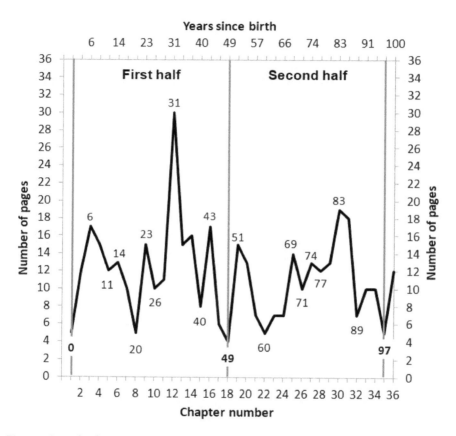

Figure 4-1: The human life cycle

## Evolutionary pressures

This methodology is only general, but the results are compelling. The diagram suggests the existence of some form of functional relationship between a person's age and generally recognised evolutionary pressures, such as the so-called 'mid-life crisis'. It also indicates some little-known phenomena, such as a meaningful difference between the first and second halves of life, and the possibility of a purpose behind the changes that occur in later life. If the diagram is correct, the implications are profound. It suggests that an individual life is somehow programmed to accommodate a number of powerful periods of change.

## The stages of life

Figure 4-2 shows these periods of change. The aging of a human being is – as before – shown along the top horizontal axis. The classifications that I have used for the different stages of evolution are the ones suggested by Richard Barrett,[40] based on the work of Professor Robert Kegan.[41] The specific details to note are: (a) the existence of energy gaps between the ages of 31 and 40, and between the ages of 83 and 89; and (b) the presence of a crisis phase between the ages of 43 and 49.

The point, however, is not the implications of these classifications (although there are many), but the fact that they fit so precisely onto the contours of the life cycle pattern. Firstly, there are two distinct halves of a natural life span. Both start with a learning (or orientation) phase and then proceed with the absorption of the implications. Both halves then end with an energy gap that marks the termination of a specific process. Most compellingly, however, is the fact that the ages at which energy trends end, or alter direction, can be used to classify the various **stages** of a human life that have been identified by psychologists.

---

[40]  One of Barrett's contributions is his focus on the second half of life, within the context of overall evolution. Richard Barrett, *A New Psychology of Human Well-Being* (Richard Barrett Fulfilling Books, London, 2016).

[41]  Kegan's work integrates three different intellectual traditions: humanistic, psychoanalytic, and developmental. It therefore puts together the findings of some of the greatest writers in psychological development. See Robert Kegan, *The Evolving Self: Problem and Process in Human Development* (Harvard University Press, Boston (Mass.), 1982).

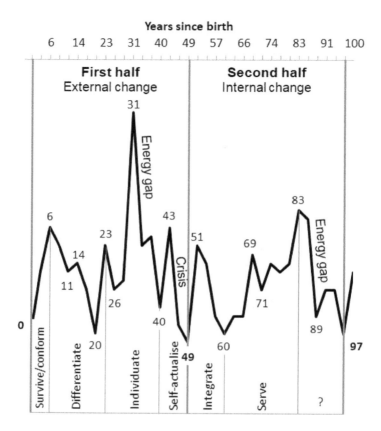

Figure 4-2: The stages of life

## The first half of life

The first half of a life span, therefore, starts with the fact of coming into existence. Consequently, the first six years or so are the natural reaction to this actuality.[42] Then, between the ages of six and 23, a person will be focused on social learning and physical growth.[43] This is the stage of separation from

---

[42]   An important indication of the accuracy of this model is the fact that a fundamental shift in consciousness occurs around the age of 6. Children become able to put themselves into the place of another, and understand what that other person might be experiencing. The ages from 0 to 6 are known as 'pre-conventional', and are essentially selfish. Ken Wilber sees evolution as consisting of a simultaneous reduction in narcissism and increase in consciousness. Ken Wilber, *A Theory of Everything* (Gateway, Dublin, 2001).

[43]   The life cycle pattern allows for a disturbance of some sort between the ages of 11 and 14. Indigenous cultures have clearly recognised that this disturbance relates to the

everyone else. Between the ages of 23 and 40, a person will develop their own way of being in the world, using (if possible) their own unique talents. This is the stage of personal individuation.

It is what happens next that is so profound. Between the ages of 40 and 49, an individual will undergo a 'mid-life crisis'. This is the stage of self-actualisation and, because it is not yet properly understood in Western societies, it can usefully be treated separately. In the meantime, it is important to note the process that is involved. The crisis is preceded by a pronounced energetic shift after the age of about 31. This shift is so subtle that it is likely to pass unrecognised by most people. However, it is an **energy gap**, and its purpose is to reorientate an individual away from outer growth towards inner realities.

This shift involves physical energies and is likely to be reflected in a reduced ability to replicate the achievements of the previous ten years. Adjustments will necessarily be made, but by the age of 40 most people will have felt – even if subconsciously – that their energies have faltered. One of the more profound insights from the diagram, therefore, is that any slowdown is only the beginning of a change.

## The mid-life crisis

The energy gap is followed by a mid-life crisis. It is widely understood that a Western woman will experience her menopause between the ages of 45 and 55, with her last menstrual period occurring on average at the age of 50. It is different with Western men, where the crisis that emerges in the late 40s and early 50s is regarded as being essentially a psychological response to failing physical capabilities. It is therefore seen as being surmountable.[44] The diagram reveals, however, that these changes are very real for men and are not confined just to women's bodies. The point is that the changes for women and men are evolutionary in nature: they arise at very specific moments in an individual's life; they incorporate a revitalisation of an individual's psychosomatic energies; and they incorporate an inner redirection of those energies.[45]

---

onset of puberty and have accordingly treated it as a time of transition from childhood to adulthood. Western cultures, on the other hand, concentrate on the transition into intellectual adulthood. Even allowing for some uncertainty about the ages shown in the diagram, most university students in the West graduate between the ages of 21 and 23.

44    See, for example, Murray Stein, *In Midlife: A Jungian Perspective* (Spring Publications, Dallas (Tx.), 1983). See also, Joanne F. Vickers and Barbara L. Thomas, *Men on Midlife* (The Crossing Press, Freedom (Ca.), 1996).

45    The mid-life crisis is so powerful that it has the potential not just to separate the first half of life from the second half, but also to create conditions for a major expansion in consciousness. See, e.g., Ken Wilber, *op. cit.*

## The second half of life

This is not the place to embark on a major consideration of personal evolution during the second half of life. Nevertheless, it is important to recognise that the revitalisation and redirection of energies will initiate a new stage of an ongoing life process. The experience of a profound inner change between the ages of 49 and 60 is designed to ensure that each person becomes less focused on the external world. Consequently, between the ages of 60 and 71, attitudes to life will change – often quite dramatically – and, thereafter, individuals are likely to become increasingly immersed in inner considerations, including the prospect of death.

This is the way that the holding field – or Mr Gurdjieff's 'third force' – seems to operate. On the one hand, profound inner growth compensates for outer physical decline; on the other hand, an individual becomes increasingly aware of the prospect of, and has time to prepare for, the biological death that is likely to occur in his or her 80s or 90s. Richard Barrett specifically sees the period after the age of around 60 as being the one where the most useful attitude to life might be that of 'service' to the whole.[46] At a very simple level, this would mean accepting that the processes that are taking place are natural. More proactively, it could mean passing on to younger people the wisdom gleaned from past experiences.

## Implications

This very simple analysis suggests three very important conclusions. The first is that Western culture's inability to recognise the mid-life change in men, and unwillingness to accept the psychological adjustment in women after they have passed through the menopause, reflects a profoundly stunted view of human nature.

Hence, despite cultural denial and outright hostility, something occurs in a human being around mid-life that has profound implications for his or her future. This is one of the implications that can be drawn from Mr Gurdjieff's concept of a third force that organises evolution.

The second conclusion is that an individual's achievements in the second half of life will depend on their personal response to this mid-life change. In particular, the initial reaction to the change, and then the subsequent incorporation of the implications of this change before the age of 60, will together form the basis for further inner evolution.

---

[46]   Richard Barrett, *op. cit.*

The third conclusion follows from this. Nature does not waste energy; it just transforms it. Therefore, the changes that arise from the first energy gap must have a purpose, even if that purpose is hidden from us. And this, in turn, implies that the second energy gap may also have an objective of which science is not – and probably cannot be – aware. This is certainly one of the conclusions that can be drawn from the adjusted form of the life cycle pressure pattern that Mr Gann hid in *The Magic Word*.

## Astrological synchronicities

The declared intention of this book is to avoid, where possible, the contentious issue of planetary influences on human behaviour. However, some of those influences are becoming increasingly difficult to ignore – particularly after the far-reaching research conducted by, for example, the philosopher Richard Tarnas.[47] The difficulty is making the jump from an observable correlation to a causal relationship. On the question of a possible transmission mechanism, scientific research still remains quiet.[48]

Nevertheless, two planetary correlations need to be mentioned. The first is the return of the planet Saturn to the same position in the astrological zodiac as it held at the time of an individual's birth. Saturn has a cycle of approximately 29 ½ years in length. A living person will therefore experience his or her first 'transit return' between the ages of 28 and 30, and the second such return between the ages of 57 and 60. Richard Tarnas finds that the Saturn return is distinctively associated with end-of-an-era effects. The impact points of this conjunction are shown in Figure 4-3. It is unlikely to be an accident that two of the major turning points in a person's energy flow occur at the ages of 31 and 60. These ages relate, respectively, to the end of youth and the end of the effects of the mid-life adjustment.

The second planetary return that seems to be deeply significant relates to the planet Uranus. Uranus has a cycle of 84 years. An initial transit, where Uranus is **opposite** its position at a person's birth,[49] occurs around the age of 42. Richard Tarnas finds that this particular conjunction is associated with creative upheavals, major breaks with tradition, and – critically – with the 'mid-life' transition. The importance of this conjunction is shown in Figure 4-3.

---

47    Richard Tarnas, *Cosmos and Psyche: Intimations of a New World View* (Plume, New York, 2007).

48    One theory is that we live in an information field consisting of mass-bearing neutrinos. The spin of some of these neutrinos will almost certainly change as they pass through various planets. In this way an individual will receive changes in his or her wider holding field and respond accordingly.

49    This conjunction is often referred to as 'Uranus opposition to natal Uranus'.

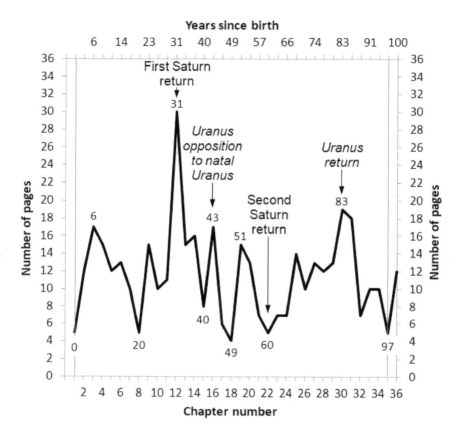

Figure 4-3: Planetary synchronicities

It seems that the Uranus transit can occur for an individual at the time of a major intellectual breakthrough,[50] or at a time when a person is already struggling to meet their own or others' expectations. In the former case, there may be a subsequent sense of anti-climax; in the latter case, there may be a feeling of release. In both cases, the result is the onset of the mid-life crisis. The final Uranus return then occurs, of course, at the age of around 84. In Figure 4-3, this synchronises with the onset of the second (and last) energy gap in an individual's life span.

---

50    Tarnas points out that the age of 42 years (+/- 1 ½ years) is associated, for example, with the breakthrough works of individuals such as Galileo Galilei, Isaac Newton, Sigmund Freud, René Descartes, Carl Jung, Albert Einstein, Emmanuel Kant, and Betty Friedan. See Richard Tarnas, *op. cit.*

## Conclusion

The life cycle pressure pattern could be a major contribution to our understanding of personal development. The close relationship between Mr Barrett's classifications and Mr Gann's life cycle pattern is consistent with the idea that Mr Gann had intended that chapter numbers in *Tunnel* could be translated into actual human ages. If so, then the life cycle pattern points to the ubiquitous operation of a natural process.

The pattern suggests that a human life is divided into two parts, that the second half is at least as important as the first half, and that the two halves are separated by a structural life change. Since the pattern applies to men as well as to women, it means that the so-called 'mid-life crisis' in the male is not just a fantasy concocted by those who have to deal with it without support. Even less is it, in itself, a personality disturbance that needs to be conquered. In fact, the pattern itself suggests that some form of deep structure process is involved.

One direct inference is that Western culture will need to accept that there is something meaningful about the mid-life transition and about the second half of life. If the first half of life is essentially physical, and the second half is more deeply psychological, what does this imply about evolution? Or about our role in that process? What adjustments might therefore be necessary for culture as a whole?

The final insight reveals a possibility that – at the moment anyway – is even more contentious. Even a cursory glance at the life cycle pattern shows that there are correlations between astronomical/astrological transits and major life changes for an individual. Western medical models presuppose the independence of rational human beings and, therefore, of their separation from cosmic cycles. But what if this is not true? What if cosmic cycles trigger observable changes in individuals? Are we participants in the workings of higher-order forces? Or are we just victims of a lower-order random process?

The significance of this analysis – which applies the life cycle pattern to a human life – is that it provides independent confirmation of the validity of the life cycle pattern itself. The human life cycle is only one use of the pattern within a huge matrix of potential applications.

# 5

# Cyclical Behaviour

## Introduction

THE CONCEPT OF a defined and predictable life cycle represents a major step forward in our understanding of life on this planet. It is quite clear, however, that any success in using it is going to depend on being able to isolate the starting point. There are a number of ways of doing this, and the relevant ideas will be revealed as the analysis progresses. For the moment, the problem is to understand how the processes of learning – defined as the inner adjustment to external change – are reflected in rhythmic oscillations. The secret is that evolutionary energies are transmitted in three main phases, that each phase encapsulates an oscillation that has its own identifiable pattern, and that all three phases have a similar duration.

## Momentum within the life cycle

Figure 5-1 shows both the life cycle format and its underlying momentum. The top part of the diagram is derived from *Tunnel*. It compares the number of pages in each chapter with the chapter number. The lower part of the diagram then shows the change in the number of pages between successive chapters. Three points are immediately apparent: firstly, the life cycle embraces three cyclical swings, or sub-cycles, each of similar duration; secondly, the mid-point of the whole life cycle does not coincide with the end of the first sub-cycle beat; and, thirdly, the learning phase within the momentum series (i.e., the black dashed line) does not immediately isolate the timing of the initiating shock.

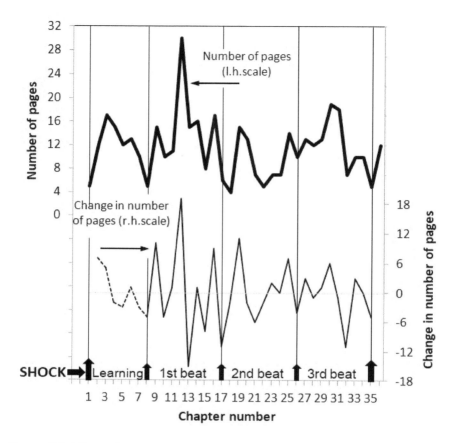

Figure 5-1: Life cycle momentum

## The cycle triad

The fact that the life cycle pattern contains three sub-cycles is of major significance. These sub-cycles are brought into being after a period of learning caused by the originating shock, and they have identical durations. This confirms the extraordinary internal coherence of the overall pattern. In practice, and as we shall see, there may well be some variability in measured duration, but such variability is unlikely to be significant. Consequently, when an analyst is looking for a life cycle and its momentum, the presence of rhythmic (if slightly variable) cycles will act as confirmation.

Each of the sub-cycles has a four-phase pattern that is unique to its location in the triad of sub-cycles. The first beat has a pronounced three-wave advance, a collapse, a three-wave recovery, and then a drop into the end-cycle low. The second beat has an initial boost, a deep contraction, an extended recovery, and then a drop into the end-cycle low. The third beat has an initial three-wave advance, a deep implosion, a sharp recovery, and then a drop into the end-cycle low.

Despite their differences, the three sub-cycles have specific parallels. Each has a distinct cycle peak; each has a pronounced intra-cycle drop that creates a low; and each has an end-cycle fall. The three sub-cycles can be averaged together to provide a behavioural locus that is in some way typical. This is shown in Figure 5-2. It is quite clear that the intra-cycle drop precludes any idea that a cycle might take the form of a sine wave.[51]

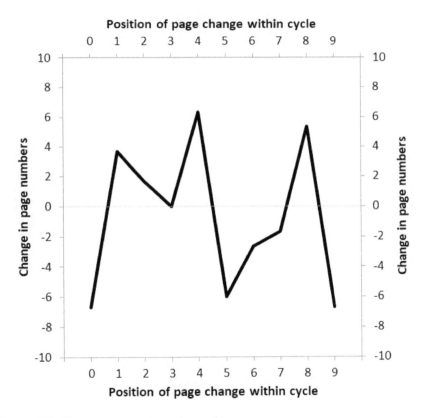

Figure 5-2: The average sub-cycle profile

51    Most analysts would assume that, if a cycle existed, it could be tracked using a sine wave. The great difficulty is that the intra-cycle downswing may be confused with the end of a cycle.

It should come as no great surprise that this average cycle has the same look to it as Mr Gurdjieff's **symbolic** enneagram that was explored in Chapter 2. We can even place the enneagram nodes on the diagram (see Figure 5-3) in order to make the comparison. This means the symbolic enneagram is an idealised model for system behaviour, once the life cycle itself has started operating. Importantly, the model explicitly includes an intra-cycle energy gap. This is represented by the move from node 8 to node 5 in Figure 5-3. Even so, the symbolic enneagram only indicates a part of total system behaviour. The life cycle is brought into being by an information/energy shock; it will need to transit through a learning process; and it will only then generate rhythmic fluctuations. But even these latter fluctuations can vary from the average.[52]

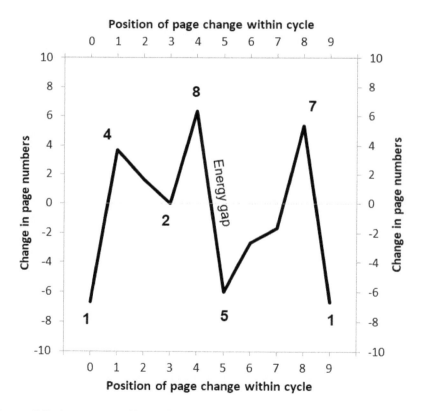

Figure 5-3: Average profile and enneagram nodes

52   Gurdjieff himself admitted that the symbolic enneagram was "incomplete and theoretical" and that "nobody could make any practical use [of it] without instruction". See Pyotr D. Ouspensky, *In Search of the Miraculous* (Harcourt, Brace & World, New York, 1949).

## Evolution and cyclical behaviour

It is often forgotten that time plays an important part in the process of evolution. At some stage, new information becomes available that makes an old set of ideas, behaviours, or circumstances untenable. However, the effects of new information have to persist long enough for the system to **know** in some way that it has to adjust. Next, the resulting internal change will spread itself over three phases. Specifically, there will be: (1) a break from the past; (2) the establishment of new structures; and (3) a testing of the system to see what works and what doesn't. [53]

The momentum of this set of changes was shown in Figure 5-1, and is now repeated in Figure 5-4. The dashed line tracks the hesitation while the system absorbs the fact that the environment has changed. The heavy line shows the energetic pressure behind the subsequent adjustment. This adjustment will extend over three segments, each of which fulfils a unique evolutionary task and each of which therefore exhibits its own distinctive pattern.

Hence, the high volatility of the first phase – and particularly the mid-cycle collapse – is consistent with its disruptive nature; the rightward bias in the second phase is a reflection of the interaction of confidence and innovation; and the deep fall in the middle of the last phase signals that the system has reached its limits. In all three cases, the end of each phase of evolution will be marked by some form of system weakness. It is, unfortunately, all too often forgotten that a period of rest is as essential to progress as is activity.

Each of the three phases has a central purpose, and can be given a label associated with that purpose. There are many descriptors that could be used, but the ones that seem the most appropriate are as shown in Figure 5-4. The cycles are named, respectively, the **Transition Cycle**, the **Transformation Cycle**, and the **Termination Cycle**.

[53]   This is similar to, but not identical with, Ken Wilber's idea of a three-stage **fulcrum**. Initially, individuals identify with a particular paradigm; then they disidentify from, and transcend, that paradigm; and, finally, individuals include and integrate the old paradigm with the next higher one. See Ken Wilber, *Integral Psychology* (Shambhala Publications, Boston (Ma.), 2000). The life cycle pattern emphasises a different aspect of the process. Individuals initially identify with an existing set of ideas. However, when new information that makes those ideas untenable becomes available, then evolution requires: (a) disidentification; (b) the laying down of the new paradigm (which may include parts of the old paradigm); and (c) trial and error with that new paradigm. Wilber's schema starts with the old era, and does not include the new era's trial and error stage.

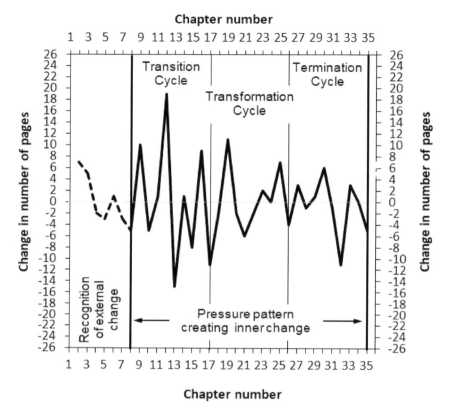

Figure 5-4: Cycle patterns within evolution

## The individual patterns

Each segment of Figure 5-4 can now be analysed separately. In the charts that follow, all will use the same vertical scales, the life cycle pattern itself will be represented by a heavy line, and the associated momentum of the life cycle will be shown as a dashed line. Using the life cycle and its momentum together is useful for two reasons. First, we can see what might be going on during each of the chart segments. It is important to note, however, that the descriptions will be only indications of underlying pressures. Contemporaneous events can force a system away from its natural path. Second, we can note divergences between the life cycle and its momentum. Such divergences are natural events at system turning points. In particular, the analyst can get some warning about a change in direction if momentum turns before the system itself. It is also true, however, that a significant time lag between a turning point in momentum and a turning point in the life cycle can create uncertainty.

## The learning cycle

The learning phase of a life cycle emerges after a change in the environment that is in some way permanent. In Chapter 3, I referred to this change as being a 'creative shock'. It is an item of information to which a system has to react.[54] Firstly, there is the question of time in relation to the system's ability to perceive the new information. There will, for example, be a problem of discriminating between a slow change and an unchanged state. Secondly, there may be a problem of available energy. The external change may not itself carry energy, but it will demand that the system uses some of its own energy to deal with the change.

In any case, if a change is registered, and it persists long enough to make a difference, then the system will have to adjust. Theoretically, this adjustment involves a change in the system's internal representations of the external world.[55] This is part of the learning process.[56]

The learning phase in evolution is shown in Figure 5-5. Firstly, there is a change in the environment. There are then two stages across which the system has to traverse: firstly, there is the initial reaction, which will take the learning system to the edge of its ability to cope; secondly, if the resulting stress lasts long enough, the fact of an external change will have to be absorbed.

The time elapse between the receipt of new information and the final stage of any subsequent inner adjustment will vary from individual system to individual system. Some warning of the ending of the stress reaction will be given by the beginning of a decline in the momentum indicator (see Figure 5-5). This is a non-confirmation of the direction of movement in the life cycle itself. But the point is that the pressure to adjust will persist until the required assimilation has finished.

---

54   Information is a "difference that makes a difference". Gregory Bateson, *Mind and Nature: A Necessary Unity* (Wildwood House, London, 1979).

55   This change in internal representations can stretch from the physical structure of a single cell organism that 'knows' what to do in its environment, to the vision of an adult person as he or she seeks to survive and move forward in the world, and on to the collective unconscious that drives the behaviour of a group.

56   It is a matter of choice whether the definition of learning is taken to include the initial stressed reaction of a system or not. In what follows, the definition of learning will be taken as both the initial stressed reaction **and** the subsequent absorption stage.

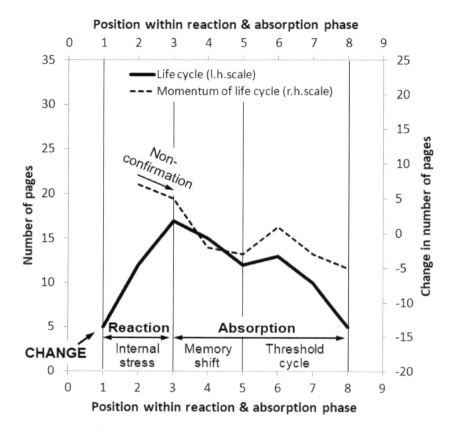

Figure 5-5: The learning phase

# The processes of learning

All self-organising systems (including systems that reflect collective human behaviour)[57] will resist a natural tendency towards disorder. So, to deal with a constantly changing environment, a system is programmed to minimise surprises.[58] For most of the time, this particular activity is hardly noticed. However, any surprise invariably involves a contraction in system behaviour as externally-orientated energy is reassigned to internal assimilation. This was

---

57  Tony Plummer, *Forecasting Financial Markets* (Kogan Page, London, 1989–2010).
58  See, e.g., Karl Friston, 'The free-energy principle: a unified brain theory?' in *Nature Reviews / Neuroscience* (Vol 11, Feb 2010, Macmillan Publishers Ltd, London, 2010).

the essential finding of Donald Hebb and of Henry Mills.[59] It seems that the assimilation process involves an interruption in a system's behaviour while information is shifted from short-term (temporary) memory to long-term (deep-structure) memory. The most obvious parallel in the material world is the reduced ability of a computer to carry out its main tasks while it is transferring data from system memory to a hard drive. It seems that every system will only have a limited amount of energy available for its activities and that some of that energy will have to be used during the learning process.[60]

The assimilation process becomes very apparent when the surprise is a large one. This is implicit in the learning patterns of Figure 2-3 and Figure 5-5. In Figure 5-5, the absorption phase is split into two parts: the initial change to long-term memory; and the threshold cycle. It is unlikely that these two parts are in any way as clearly differentiated from each other as the diagram suggests – in particular, the upgrading of long-term memory will continue into the threshold cycle. But there are a number of reasons for making sure that the threshold cycle is clearly identified: firstly, my research indicates that a muted rise followed by a sharp fall is exactly the shape of adjustment that occurs in collective behaviour; secondly, this particular stage of the learning process generates some form of external evidence that the learning is almost completed; and thirdly, the threshold cycle is the boundary beyond which the full effects of the system's learning will begin to make themselves felt.

## The Transition Cycle

Once a system has learnt that the environment has changed, it will enter a cycle that takes that change for granted and ensures that dependency on the old environment is reduced. This is the Transition Cycle, and its profile is shown in Figure 5-6. Once the cycle has been completed, it transmits two very important facts. Firstly, it signals the presence of new information in the system. The explosive three-wave rise into a peak indicates that the system has learnt that there has been a change in its environment. Secondly, the duration of the Transition Cycle will be reproduced in the subsequent Transformation and Termination Cycles. Consequently, it is possible to estimate when each of these latter two cycles will end. This, in turn, indicates when the whole life cycle is likely to finish.

---

59    Donald Hebb, *The Organisation of Behaviour* (John Wiley, New York, 1949) and Henry R. Mills, *Teaching and Training* (Macmillan Press, London, 1967).
60    In the process of learning, a system that is already low on energy will probably exhibit a larger contraction in its ability to perform standard tasks than would a system that starts with a surfeit of energy.

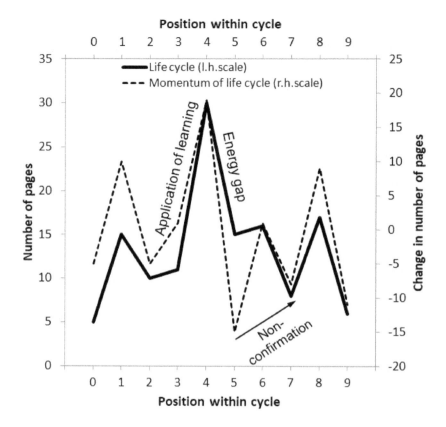

Figure 5-6: The Transition Cycle

In effect, a completed Transition Cycle locks the whole life cycle in place. It is even possible to work backwards and identify the approximate location in time of the information shock that created the whole life cycle. The prior reaction and absorption phase forms slightly under 21% of the whole life cycle, or 26% of the Transition, Transformation, and Termination Cycles taken together. If we know the total duration of the latter three cycles, then we can estimate where the life cycle actually began.

The Transition Cycle also provides some critical information about the nature of trauma. The cycle is characterised by the presence of an **energy gap**. This is the first such gap in a life cycle, and it has the potential to provide a full-blooded disruption. The momentum indicator in Figure 5-6 shows just how vicious the energy gap can be and, once it has started, it cannot be stopped or avoided.

Consequently, even after the energy gap seems to have run its course – in, for example, a stock market crash – the system still has to recuperate from the shock. This is why any recovery in the system (which can partly be anticipated by a non-confirmation of the system's energy index) does not signal the end of an adjustment. As we have already seen in the case of a male mid-life crisis, any recovery may translate into an end-cycle trauma.

## The Transformation Cycle

Having separated from the old structure – or at least from those parts that are redundant – the system can move on to the process that lays down the changes for the new era. This is the Transformation Cycle, and it is shown in Figure 5-7. It is the primary vehicle for innovation, and is thus associated with new structures.

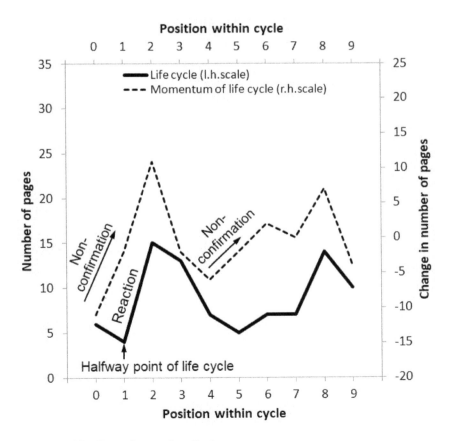

Figure 5-7: The Transformation Cycle

The Transformation Cycle has a number of distinctive characteristics. Firstly, the cycle includes the halfway point of the whole life cycle. In Mr Gann's pattern the actual low that marks the halfway point is the **lowest** level of the whole life cycle. This implies that Mr Gann intended it to stand out. Obviously, once this point has been reached, it can be used to validate both the starting date and the likely end date of the whole life cycle.

Importantly, the low can be anticipated by an improvement in the momentum indicator that occurs between the start of the Transformation Cycle and the mid-point of the life cycle. However, it is important to note that the associated divergence between the two types of cycle injects some uncertainty into the performance of whatever constitutes the system. Sometimes activity will follow the trajectory of the life cycle but sometimes it will follow the momentum index.

Secondly, the energy gap in the prior Transition Cycle, together with the aftermath of that gap and the trauma that produces the halfway point in the life cycle, generate a stimulus to which the system has to adjust. The difference this time is that the stimulus is internal, rather than external.

Thirdly, the system still has to go through a process of learning. The system has to recognise that the energy gap and its aftermath created new changes that are permanent. There is thus a period of adjustment that is necessary before the system can respond cleanly to the new stimuli. This involves the reappearance of an archetypal learning pattern. Again, the ending of the assimilation associated with this pattern can be anticipated by an improvement in the momentum indicator.

## The Termination Cycle

I have called the third cycle in the triad the Termination Cycle. This final cycle is shown in Figure 5-8. It is actually a cycle of **trial and error**. The cycle's initial function is to maximise the use of the structural innovations that were introduced in the previous Transformation Cycle. It does not rely on new innovations. So, although the early part of the cycle will appear to be quite dynamic, it will in fact be speculative. This exhausts the system's energy and, as a result, there is an **energy gap**. This second energy gap sets in motion the processes that terminate the whole life cycle.

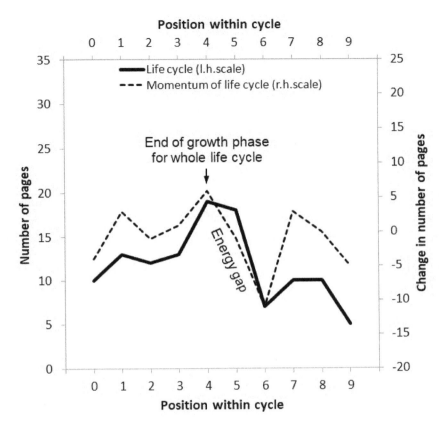

Figure 5-8: The Termination Cycle

On this analysis, the second energy gap represents the terminal phase of the system. At some point during this phase the system will finish; it will, in effect, die. This death may be literal, or it may be metaphorical as other forces in the system assume a more dominant influence; but it can be anticipated. The second energy gap does not just arrive as an accident. This has profound implications for analysing economic activity and stock markets.

## Conclusion

It bears repeating that Mr Gann's pattern has profound implications for our understanding of natural systems. A life cycle comes into being when there is a change in a system's environment. Such a change has to persist long enough for the recipient system/organism to recognise that a change in the environment has occurred. However, once the system has learnt that a change is permanent, three evolution-orientated cycles will develop. I have called these cycles the Transition Cycle, the Transformation Cycle, and the Termination Cycle respectively. All have similar durations, all have clear peaks and significant intra-cycle lows, but the average shape of the three cycles nevertheless conforms to Mr Gurdjieff's symbolic enneagram cycle.

Despite these similarities, all three cycles have unique patterns that are related to their function within the context of evolution: the first cycle separates part or all of a system away from its previous structure; the second cycle lays down the innovations that will determine the form of the new structure; and the third cycle uses that new structure to its maximum before death occurs.

The whole life cycle is divided into two halves: the first half begins with an external information shock; the second half begins with an internal one. In both cases, a learning process is triggered. Once this process is completed a system can move along its path of least resistance. This ease of movement inevitably depletes the system's energy reserves. Simply put, the system's energy becomes exhausted towards the end of the first half of the life cycle, and towards the end of the second half.

# 6

## The Life Cycle In US Equities, 1907–74

## Introduction

THE IDEA OF a life cycle can be applied to the phenomenon of financial markets. This not only emphasises the fact that financial markets are dominated by collective – rather than individual – behaviour, it also means that each major turning point can to some extent be anticipated.

In this chapter, we shall look in very general terms at the long-term life cycles that have been driving the US equity market since around the beginning of the 20th century. It will be shown that, apart from a very limited number of exceptions, major turning points in equities can be explained by significant inflexions in the relevant life cycle. This is particularly true of energy gaps, and the end-phases of the evolutionary sub-cycles that drive the life cycle.

## Energy gaps and sub-cycles

The importance of the energy gaps in a life cycle cannot be overstated. The first energy gap will help to lock the whole life cycle in place, while the second one will warn of the completion of an evolutionary process. When applied to financial markets, these two phenomena place a completely different perspective on the alleged randomness of traumatic events. Financial crashes are not mere accidents, but are part of a systemic process. There are, of course, differences: the first energy gap usually reflects conditions in a particular market, or type of market; the second energy gap, however, will signal the need for wider change. This is the primary difference, for example, between the equity crash of 1987 and the global financial crisis of 2007–09.

In the interim, there are likely to be downdrafts in financial asset prices towards the end of each of the life cycle's three sub-cycles. As we shall see, there is a noticeable variability between the conditions that are involved in each cycle, and hence in the response of the market. The final phase of the Transition Cycle, for example, may be subdued by the impact of a prior crash; the drop at the end of the Transformation Cycle is likely to be driven by the need to reduce market excesses rather than any weakness within the life cycle itself; and the very last downswing in the Termination Cycle will depend on the degree to which the prior financial crisis has been able to eliminate underlying problems.

## Theory into practice

When applying a life cycle to financial market speculation, it is important to recognise that it cannot easily be used for short-term trading. Its main use will be to provide perspective on a market, to indicate which stage of a long-term process a market is negotiating, and therefore to pinpoint the underlying trend. There are also a number of practical considerations that have to be taken into account.

Firstly, the relationships between the evolutionary stages are more rigid in theory than in practice. This is particularly true over very long time periods. Consequently, the Transition, Transformation, and Termination Cycles may vary from each other in terms of duration.

Secondly, contemporaneous pressures may encourage market behaviour to deviate from the life cycle pattern. This is unlikely to persist for significant time periods, but it means that the life cycle should be treated as a **pressure pattern** rather than as an inflexible blueprint.

Thirdly, the start and end points of a life cycle do not necessarily appear on a chart as precise moments in time. Life cycle starting dates, for example, may emerge in the context of a large matrix of different influences, which then combine to form an information shock. Furthermore, the start and end dates of a particular life cycle may merge into the movements created by the death of a prior life cycle and/or the birth of a new one.

And, fourthly, during the initial learning period (when a market is reacting to an information shock), the direction of change in a market index may not necessarily correlate with the initial rise in the life cycle pattern. Often, of course, it does. However, the initial market reaction to an information shock may just indicate an impact from that shock; it need not reflect the forthcoming direction of change. This sometimes needs interpretation.

## Locking a life cycle in place

Despite these limitations, the presence of a life cycle is usually very clear. The first task – always – is to isolate those periods that encapsulate a genuine crash. The point is that a crash and its preceding bubble will identify the presence of a Transition Cycle within a life cycle. All that is then necessary is to stretch or contract the life cycle pattern (which is easy enough using modern computer technology) so that: (a) the peak of the bubble corresponds to a market high; (b) the crash corresponds to the first energy gap; and (c) at least one subsequent bout of market weakness corresponds to a downswing in the appropriate sub-cycle. This last criterion is, of course, much easier when it relates to the second energy gap within an historical data set.

The accuracy of the overall correlation can then be confirmed by considering whether or not other oscillations within the life cycle correspond to actual fluctuations in the market. In this way, it is possible to identify a life cycle pattern that correlates with market behaviour.

## The Dow Jones Industrial Average

The Dow Jones Industrial Average (hereafter, DJIA) is an index of the 30 stocks that are assumed to track the US economy.[61] The index started in May 1896, and therefore has a long history. Unfortunately, it suffers from problems that were not envisaged when it was brought into being. Each stock in the index is weighted by price rather than by market capitalisation, and the index itself has to be reduced by a divisor to compensate for stock splits. Nevertheless, it is one of the most closely-watched and widely-cited indices.

## The DJIA'S 1907–74 life cycle

Quite obviously, a valid life cycle will have to register the influence of the 1929 Wall Street Crash. In Figure 6-1, the heavy line shows the behaviour of the DJIA from late 1896 to mid-1982. The thin line then shows the five-year percentage rate of change in the DJIA over the same period. No single momentum indicator is ever ideal, but a five-year change has the advantage of downgrading the role of short-term fluctuations in the determination of longer-term trends. Overlaid on these two time series is a dashed line, which is the life cycle of an as-yet-undefined influence on the DJIA.

As presented, inflexions in the life cycle coincide with: the low of August 1921, which introduced the stock bubble of the Roaring Twenties; the high

---

61    The stocks are subjectively picked by the editors of the *Wall Street Journal*.

of September 1929, which tipped over into the Wall Street Crash; and the high of June 1937, which anticipated the last traumatic equity fall of the Great Depression. In other words, the life cycle pattern catches the Wall Street Crash very well.

Moving forwards and backwards, the life cycle pressure pattern seems to finish at around the end of the 1973–74 inflation catastrophe, and to begin at around the end of the 1906–07 equity collapse. This implies that the proposed pattern fits the evidence very well. There are obviously some discrepancies. For example, the halfway point of the life cycle does not – as presented – coincide with the March/April 1942 low in the DJIA. We shall have to look at these a little more closely as we progress.

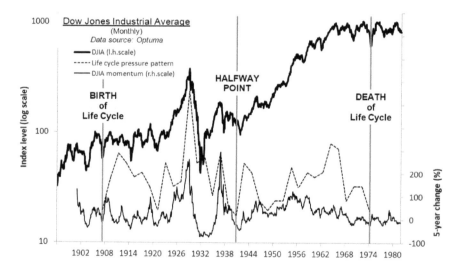

Figure 6-1: The DJIA, 1896–1982

# The 1907–21 learning phase

If we extrapolate backwards, we can estimate the start and end points of the learning phase of the proposed life cycle. Figure 6-1 suggests that this phase probably started sometime towards the end of the equity bear of 1906–07. The pattern then suggests that the subsequent reaction and assimilation period lasted until the late summer of 1921. After this, of course, there was a massive bubble. So what was it exactly that the learning entailed?

The insight is that the start (or birth) of the life cycle occurred after the 1906–07 financial panic. This panic involved a contraction in the money supply, and a near-50% collapse in stocks, as the banking system retrenched. Interestingly, this was the second major fall in the space of four years. There had been a fall of about 38% in 1903. It is highly likely that the cumulative impact of the 1903 and 1907 crises lay behind the establishment in December 1913 of the US Federal Reserve System.[62] Moreover, both the 1903 fall in the DJIA and the subsequent 1906–07 collapse were widely seen as being 'rich man's' panics. This suggests that the market's subliminal learning was that the Fed had been established in order to avoid any future banking catastrophes.

## The 1915–21 Threshold Cycle

The newly-established Fed did not, however, eliminate bear phases from the DJIA. In fact, between October 1919 and August 1921, the DJIA fell by around 44%. This fall was (again) related to the behaviour of monetary growth. In every month between late 1920 and late 1921, US money supply (as measured by M2)[63] contracted. By September 1921, the 12-month change was negative by almost 9%. It would be easy enough to argue that the Federal Reserve had made a mistake.[64] However, this is by no means the whole story; something else may have been at work.

To understand this, we need to take a closer look at the learning phase at the start of this particular life cycle. This is shown in Figure 6-2, where the DJIA itself is shown as the thick line, and the archetypal profile of the learning phase is shown as the dashed line. The end of any learning period is characterised by a Threshold Cycle (see Chapter 3). Such a cycle usually starts with a recovery in the index being tracked, and then falls sharply. Mostly, the pattern of the index coincides with the pattern of the life cycle; but sometimes it does not.

The purpose of the Threshold Cycle, particularly during the final fall, is to alter collective expectations about the future. The signal that such a change has taken place occurs when there is an external event that concretises the hidden learning. This is exactly what happened.

---

62  This phenomenon is covered again in Chapter 10.
63  M2 essentially consists of notes, coins and easily accessible time deposits. These days, the M2 aggregate also includes money market funds and savings deposits.
64  See, for example, Christina Romer, 'Does Monetary Policy Matter? A New Test in the Spirit of Friedman and Schwartz', *NBER Macroeconomics Annual* (NBER, Cambridge (MA), 1989).

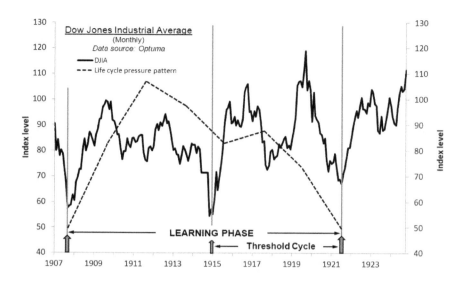

Figure 6-2: The 1907–21 learning phase

In March 1921 – towards the end of the Threshold Cycle – Warren Harding became the 29th president of the United States. His Budget Director Charles Dawes continued with the budget cuts started by the previous Administration,[65] and his Treasury Secretary Andrew Mellon introduced major cuts in private sector taxes. This latter made the difference. It emphasised that the prevailing thrust of economic analysis was both smaller government and laissez-faire.

Under these circumstances, the Fed would not have been expected to counteract any immediate effects on the private sector of cuts in public sector spending; it could concentrate instead on dealing with inflation. Consequently, the idea that the Fed would stabilise the system in the event of a banking crisis became inextricably intertwined with the conviction that the Fed's monetary policy would not focus on short-term economic growth.

## The Transition Cycle

The switch between the public to the private sectors under Warren Harding helps to explain the strength of the subsequent economic and financial recovery. In late 1921, the DJIA signalled the necessary change in mood by reversing direction and, in the subsequent eight years, the index advanced by just over

---

[65]   The previous Administration was led by Woodrow Wilson.

500%.[66] Over the same period, the monetary aggregate M2 rose in more or less a straight line by between 45% and 50%. Overall, the economy lived up to its appellation of the Roaring Twenties.

Unfortunately, this behaviour typifies the first half of a Transition Cycle. It creates the excesses that can only be unwound by an energy gap. This **first** energy gap in the life cycle is shown in Figure 6-3. It was the infamous Wall Street Crash. In fact, the Crash itself was only the first part of a three-phase collapse in the DJIA. The first stage (3 September to 13 November) involved a fall of just under 50%; the second stage (13 November 1929 to 16 April 1930) embraced a rally of just over 50%; and the final stage (16 April 1930 to 8 July 1932) witnessed a collapse of 86%.[67] It is arguable that the energy gap should have ended in 1931. However, it didn't do so, which suggests the presence of other influences. Overall, between the high on 3 September 1929 and the eventual low on 8 July 1932, the DJIA fell by almost 90%. Indeed, at its low in 1932, the DJIA was below the worst level of 1921.

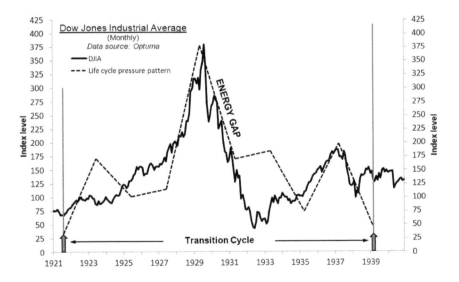

Figure 6-3: The 1921–39 Transition Cycle

---

66   A movement of 500% implies the influence of the octave ratio, 50:100.
67   Movements of 50% and 86% also suggest that the octave ratio, 50:100, was exerting an influence. See Appendix II.

# Monetary policy and the role of the Fed

It is an important fact that the same profile applied to US money supply. I shall cover this in a little more detail in Chapter 10, which deals with the Great Depression. In the meantime it is relevant that, between its high in autumn 1929 and its eventual low in spring 1933, M2 dropped by about 38%. In early 1933, the level of M2 was lower than it had been in 1921. This means that, contrary to the understanding that had developed between investors and the Fed during the equity bubble, the authorities had actually allowed the US money supply to implode during the subsequent equity collapse. The significant point is that the 1921–1932 bubble-and-crash phenomenon involved a passive monetary policy, rather than a proactive one. The Fed was brought into being shortly after of the 1907 panic; its tolerant monetary policy supported the 1921–29 bubble; and its laissez-faire attitude facilitated the 1929–32 equity collapse.

In retrospect, the Fed's behaviour over the period can be classified as being dangerous. It did not adequately differentiate between changes that left the economic environment unaffected (to which it need not respond) and changes that actively altered the environment (to which it should respond). But it is also true that, at that stage, the Fed was inexperienced. Monetary policy errors were inevitable as the Fed learnt about the nature of its power. In fact, its failures during the 1929–32 period were part of the reason for the establishment in 1933 of the Federal Open Market Committee (FOMC). The FOMC was given the task of establishing an appropriate monetary policy.

# The aftermath of the first energy gap

We can now have a closer look at the sequence of events that followed the Wall Street Crash. Figure 6-3 reveals that the first energy gap in a life cycle is followed by two specific developments. The first is that there is a recovery of some sort, but this is then followed by a retracement. This is why the energy gap itself is never the end of the system response to the preceding bubble. The second is that, as the life cycle moves into its second half, a learning process develops. Sometimes the troubles generated by the Transition Cycle have to carry over into Transformation Cycle; but, at other times, this is not the case. Either way, the tone is set for the subsequent shift in objectives within the life cycle. This is why the second half of the life cycle can include a genuinely sustainable trend.

# The 1937–38 recession

This set of insights helps to explain the emergence of the 1937–38 drop in the DJIA and the associated recession. Figure 6-3 showed that the DJIA began to recover after 1932, but that – not surprisingly – the rally was hesitant. After

July 1934, it became more persistent and, by early March 1937, the DJIA had recovered by 382% from the 1932 low.[68] This was, however, the high for about five years, because there was another monetary shock. Having previously allowed gold inflows to inflate the money supply, the US Treasury Department began in December 1936 to sterilise such inflows. Not surprisingly, the money supply stopped growing, the US economy dropped back into a recession, and the DJIA fell sharply. Between 10 March 1937 and 31 March 1938, the DJIA lost 50%.[69]

This sequence of events matches the life cycle as presented in Figure 6-3. Specifically, the 1937–38 drop in the DJIA coincided with the end phase of the Transition Cycle. It also coincided with an important energy gap within the context of a regular 36-year oscillation in the economy (see Chapters 9 and 10). This energy gap – which explains the 1937–38 economic recession – started the ending process of one socio-economic era and began the movement towards a new one. It also needs to be pointed out, however, that the character of the new socio-economic era was dependent on the fact that the authorities had been pursuing a relatively passive monetary policy. Without such an approach, the new era might have looked completely different.

## The second half of the life cycle

Normally, there is a period between the start of the Transformation Cycle and the halfway point of that life cycle when the system has a significant degree of flexibility. In the case of the DJIA's 1907–74 life cycle, not only did equities fall during this period, but they continued to fall even after the halfway stage. One of the issues at the time was the dislocation caused by WWII. This was sufficiently unusual to mean that there is no need to adjust the life cycle profile to take account of the weakness in the DJIA.

Even so, the original profile in Figure 6-1 indicates that the final downswing of the archetypal Transformation Cycle does not coincide fully with the 1956–57 bear phase in the DJIA. This suggests that the duration of the Transformation Cycle needs to be increased and that the duration of the Termination Cycle needs to be reduced, while leaving the original total length of the two cycles unchanged.

These adjustments are made in Figure 6-4, which shows the second half of the 1907–74 life cycle. The overall length of the second half of the life cycle remains

---

68    A 382% change implies the influence of the golden ratio, 38.2:61.8.
69    At the same time, the Fed increased reserve requirements for banks in an attempt to reduce the build-up of excess reserves, and President Hoover introduced higher taxes (including payroll taxes) in order to "spread the burden". Neither was appropriate in highly sensitive economic conditions.

unchanged at just over 33½ years, but the length of the Transformation Cycle is increased from 17¾ years to about 18⅔ years, and the length of the Termination Cycle is accordingly reduced from 17¾ years to around 17 years. The average of these two cycles is 17⅔ years, which is identical to the length of the Transition Cycle. On very long cycles, small adjustments to cycle lengths are not only normal, but are probably essential. Having made them, the correlation between the DJIA and its ideal pathway becomes even more compelling.

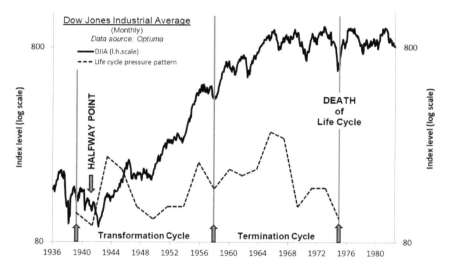

Figure 6-4: Second half of the 1907–74 life cycle

## The Transformation Cycle

At the halfway point of the DJIA's life cycle, in spring 1941, WWII was already underway. Consequently, the DJIA was unusually weak. Nevertheless, after the halfway point, there was a distinct change. The DJIA rose sharply, and did not subsequently lose much ground. This was the learning stage of the Transformation Cycle, and it is likely that investors and the authorities were absorbing the fact that monetary policy in the first half of the life cycle had been profoundly disruptive. It is highly likely, therefore, that by June 1949 the collective learning was that the authorities had to be much more careful in their approach to monetary policy. In effect, this implied a persistent monetary stimulus.

## The trend in the Transformation Cycle

After the learning phase has finished, the main feature of a Transformation Cycle is likely to be a sustainable trend. Consequently, between June 1949 and August 1956, the DJIA rose with very little interruption from an intra-day low of 162.51 to an intra-day high of 523.33 – a rise of 226%. However, a sustained advance in an equity market almost always produces investor excesses. So, when end-cycle pressures began to exert an influence after August 1956, the DJIA began to drop away. It is no accident that the weakness was anticipated by the life cycle profile, and coincided with the onset of an economic recession. By the end of the Transformation Cycle in December 1957, the DJIA had fallen by 19%.

## The Termination Cycle

Once the Transformation Cycle has finished, an equity market will likely enter a much more speculative phase. The **fundamental** forces that drove the uptrend during the Transformation Cycle will by now have become exhausted, or at least slowed significantly. Consequently, equities have to rely on their own momentum and on a monetary stimulus. In the background, however, long-term momentum (however calculated) will no longer confirm the market's strength. Once this happens, equities become vulnerable and will almost certainly encounter bouts of selling pressure.

The real danger, though, materialises after the life cycle itself turns down. This simultaneously signals the natural end – although perhaps not the **final** end – of the equity upswing and the withdrawal of any remaining fundamental support. There may not be an immediate negative reaction from equities. Indeed, it is one of the features of the idealised life cycle that its final downswing does not start dramatically. This allows the authorities to provide monetary support for equities – which is what happened after 1966. But the point is that the real economy will have lost its natural dynamism, and will probably be heading into a recession. When this becomes obvious, equities will fall sharply.

## The second energy gap

Figure 6-1 showed that the life cycle pattern that began in October 1907, and then harmonised with the DJIA's bubble-and-crash, also finished in the first half of the 1970s. In fact, it is likely that the life cycle's terminal juncture occurred in late 1974.

The situation is shown in Figure 6-5. The DJIA fell in 1966 after the life cycle had turned down. This is not normally the stage where the final energy gap materialises, so the DJIA rose again. In fact, the life cycle pattern suggested that the energy gap should have started in late 1967, but the downswing was delayed until December 1968. At this stage, the DJIA started to respond to the pressure pattern, and it entered its end-of-cycle bear phase. Three waves were involved: the 1968–70 bear itself; a highly speculative 1970–73 rally; and the 1973–74 collapse. It seems that, because of the Vietnam War, the 1970–73 period involved a stimulus that the DJIA could not resist. That stimulus was inflationary, and the result was the 1973–74 collapse. The bear started in January 1973 and ended in December 1974, and caused the DJIA to fall by just under 47%. It seems that the end-of-cycle trauma occurred in the **aftermath** of the second energy gap, rather than during the energy gap itself. Nevertheless, it was a valid part of the life cycle that began in 1907.

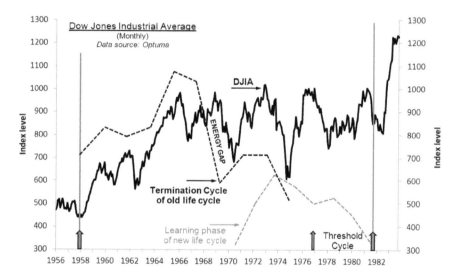

Figure 6-5: The second energy gap

## Implications of the second energy gap

This brings into focus four very important aspects of the final energy gap. The first of these is that the system will have mutated after the first energy gap, so that the second gap applies to an evolved form of the system.

The second aspect of the second energy gap is that the system's 'death' can occur any time after the life cycle profile starts to turn down. This seems to be what happened in the late 1960s and early 1970s.

The third aspect of the 1968–70 energy gap in the DJIA was that it might not have worked immediately because it needed to harmonise with two other major developments of the period in output and in prices. Between 1970 and 1978, US industrial production was in the Termination Cycle of its own triad of 10- to 11-year cycles that began in 1946 (see Chapter 9). This suggested that output was due to enter an energy gap sometime between 1973 and 1975. At the same time, US wholesale prices were in the Transition Cycle of a triad of 12- to 14-year cycles that started in 1961 (see Chapter 12). This implied that prices would reach a major peak sometime between 1973 and 1975. This conjunction of events certainly allowed that the DJIA would have to face a trauma in 1973–75.

Finally, end-of-cycle energy gaps can in themselves be the trigger for a new life cycle (see Chapter 7). The 1968–70 bear, and then the 1973–74 collapse, would have initiated a learning process that was linked to the need to control inflation. This had profound implications in the years that followed.

## The evolution of the Federal Reserve

The experience of 1966 to 1974 reveals one of the important characteristics of final energy gaps. This is that – somehow – the activities in the various sectors of the economy become sufficiently coordinated to condense into a widespread problem. In the case of monetary policy and the DJIA, the inherent official bias towards low interest rates and stimulating the real economy overruled the dangers of inflation – until it was too late.

One inference is that the DJIA's life cycle, which began in 1907 and ended in 1974, had a great deal to do with the joint evolution of monetary policy, economic activity, and monetary inflation. After the first energy gap, the Fed was forced to recognise that it could control the real economy. At the second energy gap, however, it was forced to realise that it also had to control inflation. In particular, the experience of the 1966–74 period confirmed that the monetary financing of government spending is ultimately inflationary.[70]

A second inference, of course, is that the authorities **reacted** to events, rather than anticipated them. This is the main reason why the initial fluctuations in the second half of a life cycle can also be seen as belonging to a learning experience.

---

70   It is, of course, arguable that economic policy had to include the financing of the war in Vietnam. But it is then also arguable that this financing ought to have come from other sources. A political decision to be involved in a war requires domestic sacrifices.

## Conclusion

The first major conclusion from this analysis is that a creative shock sets in motion a predictable response, which has a life cycle. This life cycle expands through time, and demonstrates the existence of some form of memory. In the case of the DJIA, the 1907–74 life cycle demonstrates a link between the two major traumas that defined it – i.e., the first and second energy gaps. The first trauma triggered a change in attitudes but, ironically, those attitudes then contributed to the second trauma. The inference is that there is a policy-related link between the equity collapse of 1929–32 and the equity contraction of 1973–74.

This brings into focus the second major conclusion from this chapter. Although the equity traumas of 1929–32 and 1973–74 differed in their magnitude and in their repercussions, both were preceded by lax monetary policies, and both were triggered by official attempts to reverse those policies. This means the life cycle that was reflected in oscillations in the DJIA between 1907 and 1974 was actually a reflection of the Federal Reserve's struggle to balance the objectives of controlling inflation and stimulating economic activity. If the Life Cycle Hypothesis is correct, then the two objectives are ultimately incompatible. After the 1929–32 experience, the authorities knew that they had to support economic activity, but the result was inflation.

The third conclusion relates to the Life Cycle Hypothesis itself. The presence of a life cycle will be obvious once the first energy gap associated with the Transition Cycle has materialised. This may then allow an estimate of the timing of the prior creative shock and, therefore, an interpretation of its influences. But a life cycle can only relate to dominant long-term influences. In the early stages of a life cycle, it is inevitable that interpretations will be subjective.

# 7

# The Life Cycle In US Equities, 1970–Present

## Introduction

THERE IS STRONG evidence that collective behaviour responds in a non-random manner to a change in the external environment. The response involves learning that the change is sufficiently long-lasting that it cannot be ignored, and then adjusting to that change by undergoing an internal mutation. The internal mutation is based on an archetypal pattern. This pattern, which is the basis of all evolution, has a distinct life cycle.

In the last chapter, I outlined persuasive evidence for the existence of such a life cycle in the DJIA between 1907 and 1974. It appears that the main driving force was the policy orientation of the Federal Reserve. The evidence from one time period is not, however, sufficient by itself. At a minimum, we need to ensure that the fundamental pattern in the DJIA reproduces itself over other time periods.

This chapter looks at the DJIA's 1970–2023 life cycle, which followed that of 1907–74. We will find that the monetary policy of the Fed is still the primary driving force. However, we will also find that – again – the life cycle reflects inflation expectations.

## A necessary comparison

Figure 7-1 compares the performance of the DJIA after 1970 with its performance between 1907 and 1974. The upper chart is the one that was shown in Figure 6-1. However, it has been slightly adjusted to reflect the comments made in Chapter 6. In both charts, the DJIA (heavy line) is measured on the left-hand vertical axis in logarithmic form, the index's momentum (thin line) is shown on the right-hand vertical scale as a five-year percentage change, and the idealised life cycle pressure pattern (dashed line) is added as a free standing schematic.

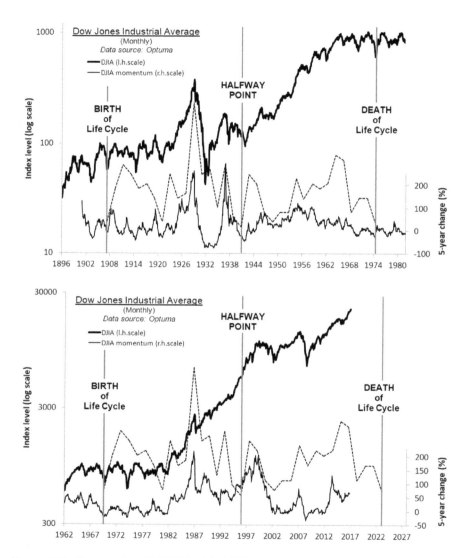

Figure 7-1: Comparing 1907–74 with 1970–present

At first sight, the DJIA's behavioural patterns are different between the two charts. However, when the archetypal life cycle profile is taken into account, the similarities start to become more obvious. The main feature of both patterns is that they include genuine equity 'crashes'. The first is the 1929 Wall Street Crash; the second is the 1987 equity crash. Both phenomena were preceded by loose monetary policies; both reflected investor over-commitment to the equity market; and both crashes were triggered by monetary tightening. The important point is that a financial crash identifies the presence of an evolution-orientated Transition Cycle.

## Locking the cycle in place

Once the presence of a Transition Cycle in the currently-evolving life cycle has thus been identified, we can lock the whole life cycle into place by aligning the pattern with the obvious oscillations in the DJIA. In Figure 6-1 of Chapter 6, we were able to use a number of inflexions in the DJIA to turn the key in the lock. In Figure 6-3, in fact, we were able to correlate the downswing at the end of the Transformation Cycle with the DJIA's 1956–57 bear phase. We can now repeat this procedure for the current life cycle.

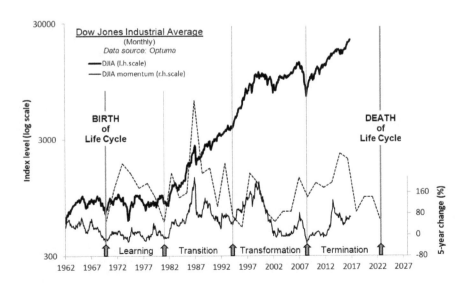

Figure 7-2: Sub-cycles in the DJIA since 1970

Figure 7-2 accordingly shows the fluctuations in the DJIA since the 1970s, aligned both with the 1987 crash and with the downswing at the end of the Transformation Cycle. For clarity, the sub-cycles (including the learning cycle) are individually identified. The diagram reveals that – astonishingly – the end of the contemporaneous Transformation Cycle was formed by the 2007–09 global financial crisis.

## The 1981–94 Transition Cycle

This, in itself, is worthy of further comment because it introduces a whole new perspective on the evolutionary forces that were (and still are) at work. In the meantime, locking the life cycle into place means that we can make some initial comments about the DJIA's 1981–94 Transition Cycle. Firstly, the effects of the characteristic 'crash' persisted beyond the initial energy gap. The aftermath can be reflected either in the index itself, or in the momentum of the index. In the case of the 1929 crash, for example, the Transition Cycle ended with the 1937–38 bear phase. In the case of the 1987 crash, on the other hand, persistent official stimuli supported the market and thereby hid the underlying fluctuations. The effect was that the Transition Cycle did not end properly until the five-year momentum indicator was able to recover. Whatever the circumstances, unfettered progress cannot be achieved until the aftermath of the first energy gap is out of the way.

Secondly, therefore, contemporaneous influences always need to be taken into account. The energy gap within the Transition Cycle does not insert a new creative drive into a system. It will certainly generate enquiry because something, somewhere, has not worked. But its basic function is to remove the energy from the prior expansion, and thereby allow the unwinding of excesses. In other words, the system has to find its own equilibrium.

## The 1970–81 learning cycle

Once the life cycle appears locked in place, we can shift our attention backwards in time, and estimate the starting point of the creative shock. Figure 7-3 relates to the first half of the current life cycle. The level of the DJIA is shown on a logarithmic scale on the left-hand vertical axis, and the momentum of the index is shown as a five-year percentage change on the right-hand vertical axis. The pattern places the initiating shock sometime in spring 1970. This is precisely when the US Fed embarked on an episode of interest rate reductions. Between May 1970 and May 1971, the effective Fed funds rate fell from above 8% to around 3¾%.

The obvious inference is that inflation was being injected into the economic and financial system. Another inference is that, at some level, the system knew it.

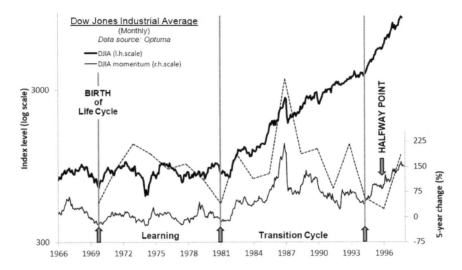

Figure 7-3: First half of current life cycle

There are two associated influences here, both related to the Fed's monetary policy. Firstly, and as we shall see in Chapter 12, the long-term US wholesale price cycle had, in 1970–72, entered the foothills of a major inflation. Secondly, in the second half of 1972, the DJIA started to ignore the implications of higher interest rates. Despite a move by the Federal Reserve to tighten monetary policy, the DJIA rose. This is **prima facie** evidence that the index had entered a highly speculative phase within the Termination Cycle of the 1907–74 life cycle.

These insights place the 1973–74 fall in the DJIA – and thus one of the important features of the new learning cycle – into a broader framework. It was not just a natural response to the Fed's belated attempts to control inflation. The sheer extent of the drop in equity prices sent a clear message to the authorities that high inflation was damaging the economic and financial system. The period from 1974 to 1981 was accordingly dominated by the ongoing assimilation of that message. Indeed, in 1979, President Jimmy Carter nominated Paul Volcker to take charge of the Federal Reserve System.[71] Mr Volcker was firmly committed to controlling inflation.

---

71    The president's nominee for the post has to be confirmed by the Senate.

# Comparing the learning cycles

It is an important fact that events during the 1970–81 learning cycle paralleled events during the 1907–21 learning cycle. Firstly, the sharp drop in the DJIA (of 47%) in 1973–74 mirrored the drop (of 44%) in 1912–14. Secondly, the bear phase of 1973–74 took place as the Vietnam War was entering its final stages, while the fall of 1912–14 took place as WWI was just beginning. Thirdly, in 1974, US wholesale prices hit a major cycle peak; in 1916, the US wholesale prices also hit a major cycle peak. Finally, towards the end of both the 1970–81 and 1907–21 learning cycles, there were definite indications that the learning had actually been completed and that the assimilation process was therefore reaching its conclusion. In 1979, President Jimmy Carter signalled the intent to control inflation by nominating as a Fed chairman someone who was prepared to contain US money growth. In the previous cycle, in 1920, President Warren Harding acted to reduce the inflationary costs of government by cutting public sector spending and reducing private sector taxation. In both cases, inflation came down – slowly in the 1970–81 learning cycle; dramatically in the 1907–21 learning cycle.

# The importance of Threshold Cycles

These correlations point to the presence of an ordered process. The timings are different, and the way the influences manifest themselves are different, but the similarities between the two learning cycles cannot be ignored. And this brings us to a particularly important aspect of the two learning cycles. In Figure 5-5, I indicated that the last phase of the learning process could be termed a Threshold Cycle. This designation is appropriate because it represents the entry point into a new era. A Threshold Cycle is usually characterised by an initial rise followed by a steep fall, and the end of that fall becomes imminent when an overt event confirms a shift in collective psychology. At this point, we know that the emotional environment has shifted.[72] Hence, the budget cuts by President Harding in 1920, and the nomination of Paul Volcker in 1979, were each in their own way definitive indications that the economic and financial system was entering a new period of evolution.

# The link between 1920 and 1979

The 1920 and 1979 end-of-learning signals could not appear more different from each other – and yet there is a way in which they are linked. Firstly, they occurred 59 years apart. This is an oblique reference to the presence of a 54-year

---

[72]   There is always a mood change at the end of an important cycle.

(Kondratyev) cycle in US wholesale prices. We will cover this in much more detail in Chapter 12 but, as should by now have become apparent, this cycle is unmistakeably linked to the Fed's monetary policies.

Secondly, the 1979 signal indicated a shift in policy objectives (from inflation to disinflation), but was nevertheless an evolutionary development from the 1920 signal. The important point here is that the Federal Reserve came into being at a time when policy decisions were based on laissez-faire – the belief that the economy should be allowed to adjust as necessary. For many years, therefore, the Fed's central stance was one of non-intervention unless there was a 1907-type financial crisis. As argued in Chapter 6, this explains why the Fed did not fight the 1920–21 recession, and it helps to explain (but not justify) why the monetary aggregates were allowed to contract in 1929–32.

On this analysis, the important signal that the 1907–1921 learning cycle was ending was not just President Harding's decision to cut public sector spending; it was also the fact that there was no related change in the Fed's policy orientation. It is difficult now, in an environment that presumes the rectitude of neo-Keynesian government intervention, to recognise that monetary policy can be neutral. However, the problem turned out not to be one of doing nothing as opposed to doing something; the problem revealed itself to be that the Fed could not distinguish in practice between economic and financial changes within an otherwise stable environment (which it could leave alone) and changes that altered the operating environment itself (which it needed to counterbalance).

There was thus a sequence of interrelated changes: the Fed came into existence (1907–13); its policy attitude meant that it remained neutral in relation to the post-WWI fiscal changes (1920–21); the monetary disaster of the 1930s (the first energy gap) obliged the Fed to be more responsive to weak output;[73] and, because of this, the Fed eventually had to deal with runaway inflation (1979). For the Federal Reserve System, the link between the end of the 1907–21 learning cycle and the end of the 1970–81 learning cycle was thus developmental. Between the two periods, there was a huge upheaval in policy objectives, involving a shift from no response to an active response.

## Second half of life cycle

Figure 7-4 covers the Transformation Cycle and the Termination Cycle. It therefore encompasses the period from November 1994 to the likely end-date of the whole life cycle in early 2023. By definition, this means that Figure 7-4

---

73   The Federal Open Market Committee (FOMC) was established in 1933. Its function was to set an appropriate monetary policy.

also covers the second half of the current life cycle. Again, the level of the DJIA is shown on a logarithmic scale, the momentum of the index is shown as a five-year percentage change, and the life cycle is shown in schematic form.

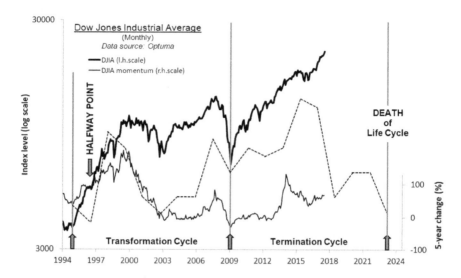

Figure 7-4: Second half of current life cycle

The first point is that the stunning correlation between the archetypal pattern of the life cycle during the Transformation Cycle and the actual behaviour of the DJIA is a direct confirmation of the power of the Life Cycle Hypothesis. Secondly, the life cycle allows for weakness in the DJIA between the start of the Transformation Cycle (in November 1994) and the halfway mark (in June 1996). In this case, the weakness did not occur; in fact, the DJIA rose strongly. Thirdly, the life cycle remained positive until just prior to the Russian debt crisis in 1998. In this sense, the life cycle pattern warned of a problem. However, the downturn in the life cycle schematic was only modest, so an ongoing reaction from the behavioural index was not essential. Here, the DJIA renewed its advance after the 1998 crisis, reaching a peak just before the life cycle turned down more sharply. The life cycle and the DJIA then fell together during the 2000–02 bear phase.

# The new learning phase

This rise and fall in the early stages of the second half of the life cycle is critically important. It involves a new bout of learning. In Chapter 6, it was argued that the comparable stage of the 1907–74 life cycle entailed an adjustment in collective attitudes to monetary policy. After the long depression of the 1930s, the Fed finally decided that it had no option other than to target output in a more proactive manner. In the current (1970–2023) life cycle, the learning seems to have mutated into a more aggressive form of this attitude. Crudely put, the collective learning between mid-1996 and late-2002 was that monetary policy was **all** that mattered.

This is certainly consistent with fundamental developments during the early part of the DJIA's Transformation Cycle. As we shall see in Chapter 9, the 1990s were characterised by a revolution in technology and in information transmission. This 'infotech' revolution was disinflationary. Consequently, inflation itself was progressively downgraded as a constraint on stimulative monetary policies.

Then, in the second half of 1999 and early 2000, three things happened: firstly, the Fed belatedly started to become concerned about inflation, and raised official interest rates; secondly, equity markets generally – and technology stocks in particular – became overstretched; and, thirdly, at a fundamental level, the infotech revolution lost some of its impetus. The immediate consequence was that technology stocks collapsed; the secondary effect was that there was a recession in 2001 and that industrial stocks fell sharply in 2001–02. The actual peak in the DJIA was in January 2000, but the market took more than a year to develop a top pattern. The biggest part of the fall (almost 38%) was between May 2001 and October 2002.

# The Transformation Cycle

The point that needs emphasising is that the 1990s rally in the DJIA and its subsequent collapse in 2000–02 occurred during the phase of the life cycle that accommodates a new learning process. In principle, this anticipates a more focused phase of evolution. Here, the learning process involved a recognition that equity market fundamentals were shifting away from considerations of value towards the consequences of changes – any changes – in monetary policy. It was this simple switch that defined the essence of the Transformation Cycle.

Moreover, the switch accounted for the subsequent behaviour of the DJIA. Between October 2002 and July 2007, and in line with the **trend** phase of the Transformation Cycle, the DJIA almost doubled. During this advance, however, the Fed actually raised interest rates (from around 1% in mid-2004 to 5¼% in mid-2007). So the important question is, why didn't equities reflect this?

One answer is that the tightening effects of Fed policy were being offset by Japanese monetary policy. Between March 2001 and March 2006, the Bank of Japan supplemented its policy of zero interest rates with quantitative easing (QE) – i.e., the purchase of government bonds (and other assets) with printed money.[74] Speculators borrowed at low Japanese interest rates, sold yen into dollars, and bought US bonds (and other assets) that had higher yields. Between January 2005 and June 2007, when this yen 'carry trade' had its greatest momentum, dollar-yen rose by 22%. For the Fed, a rising dollar might have indicated a successful tightening process. In fact, not only was that tightening being undermined, but each rise in US interest rates created a greater stimulus. Whether the authorities liked it or not, US monetary policy had become integrated with global monetary policy. The eventual financial crisis was the worst in living memory.

The ending of the Bank of Japan's bond buying programme in 2006 may well have been a necessary precursor for this financial crisis. In any case, higher US interest rates did eventually have an effect. The US housing market turned down, and the yen carry trade went into reverse. Between July 2007 and March 2009, the DJIA more than halved. In other words, the excesses generated by the trend in the Transformation Cycle resulted in a massive correction.[75]

## The Termination Cycle

Once the Transformation Cycle has ended, the Termination Cycle starts. This cycle is reproduced in Figure 7-5 where, as in previous charts, the level of the DJIA (heavy line) is shown on a logarithmic scale on the left-hand vertical axis, the momentum of the index (thin line) is shown as a five-year percentage change on the right-hand vertical axis, and the archetypal pattern of the Termination Cycle itself (dashed line) is overlaid on both. The whole cycle runs from the crisis-induced low of the DJIA in March 2009 to early 2023.

[74] Purchases are made by the central bank, and newly printed money becomes available to the bond seller. The seller's balance sheet has cash rather than bonds; the central bank holds bonds rather than newly-created cash. This brings yields down, or keeps them low.
[75] The Life Cycle Hypothesis reveals an important distinction between the overall fall in the DJIA in 2007–09 and events such as, for example, the Wall Street Crash of 1929. The former ended the process of building a workable structure, whereas the latter signalled the need for a new structure.

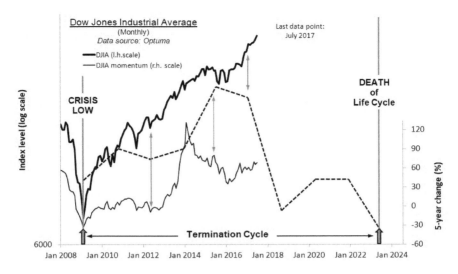

Figure 7-5: Termination Cycle, 2009-2023

The onset of a Termination Cycle does not mean that the flow of new ideas that characterised the Transformation Cycle just stops. Nevertheless, that flow definitely slows – often quite markedly. The first half of the Termination Cycle is therefore energised, not by new ideas, but by the commitment to old (or existing) ideas. This implies the dominance of emotionally-laden beliefs. Moreover, these beliefs become more focused as a trend progresses.[76] In a financial market such as the equity market, this can make the Transition Cycle highly speculative.

Most tellingly, the DJIA rose as the Fed reflated. Fed funds, which had been 5¼% as the collapse in the DJIA started in mid-2007, were at only notional levels by end-2008. Moreover, they stayed there, boosted by official purchases of government bonds.[77] The overriding presumption was that the global financial crisis of 2007–09 was a deflationary event, and that inflation was not therefore an issue. In effect, a naturally speculative environment was unnaturally inflamed by official policy.

---

[76]   The narrowing of the belief matrix is one of the identifying features of crowd behaviour. See Tony Plummer, *Forecasting Financial Markets* (Kogan Page, London, 1989–2010).
[77]   This is quantitative easing. See note 74.

## A pressure pattern

It is important to remember that the archetypal life cycle pattern (and its sub-cycles) cannot automatically be used for short-term timing. First, life cycles interact with each other over various time frames. This means that shorter cycles will be distorted by longer ones. Second, contemporary events will have an immediate impact and will pull collective behaviour away from the pathway indicated by the life cycle.

A life cycle pattern therefore shows the **tendencies** within an evolutionary process, not a precise pathway. Consequently, actual trends in the DJIA can turn either before or after the moment identified by the archetypal pattern. Nevertheless, the life cycle pattern will confirm that a new trend will persist until around the time of the next turning point in the pattern.

## An energy gap?

The rising phase of the Termination Cycle probably peaked in spring 2015. The initial downswing of such a cycle is modest. This allows for contemporaneous influences – such as, in this case, monetary reflation – to create a divergence from the schematic pathway. The fact remains, however, that the Termination Cycle entered the last energy gap of the 1974–2023 life cycle in late 2016. The obvious question is, why has the DJIA not yet fallen? Moreover, what are the longer-term implications?

One of a number of fundamental answers to the question is that global monetary policy has become so integrated that one country cannot make policy decisions that conflict with those of others. At the time of writing, continental Europe, the UK and Japan are still pursuing expansionist monetary policies, and it is noticeable that the US has had to resist an aggressive tightening because of the potential effects on financial markets. But this is only a part of the answer. Another part of the answer is that the DJIA's life cycle may not apply just to the direction of change in US equity markets; it may also apply to the structure of beliefs that lie behind monetary policy.

## Monetary policy and innovation

This chapter has outlined sufficient evidence that US monetary policy has been one of the main driving forces behind the DJIA. In the early stages of the 1974–2023 life cycle, the distinction between such policy and the performance of the DJIA was largely unnecessary. Inflation progressively came under control and, for a significant period of time, the Fed attempted to pursue a non-inflationary monetary policy. The technological revolution of the 1990s changed that; the supply of new products, based on information flows, introduced non-monetary disinflation into the economic environment.

Unfortunately, the Federal Reserve seems not to have taken full account of the implications of this phenomenon. It assumed, in effect, that the technological stimulus would be continuous. As we shall see in Chapter 14, however, this was not the case. The economic slowdown of the early 2000s reflected a deceleration in the arrival of new digital hardware onto the markets. The official response was a monetary stimulus. Such a stimulus cannot, of course, trigger innovation. So, inevitably, excess money has found its way into the equity market.

## Implications

This means that there is now a mismatch between equities and the real economy. But the mismatch is asymmetric: on the one hand, the DJIA is responding primarily to monetary policy, rather than to fundamental economic trends; on the other hand, a fall in equities is seen as being the likely cause of a deep recession. The presumption – just as in the 1920s – is that the Fed will provide a safety net.

The DJIA's life cycle has for many years been tracking financial conditions within an environment of disinflation/deflation. The energy gap implies that containing inflation is no longer a genuine goal. Indeed, the rise in the DJIA implies that another stimulus may occur in due course.

## Conclusion

This chapter has surveyed the behaviour of the DJIA since the official reflation that started in spring 1970. This was the creative shock for a life cycle that is currently still evolving, and that is due to end sometime in 2023. The shock arrived in the relatively early stages of the war in Vietnam, so it was not immediately obvious that the official stimulus was as inflationary as it turned out to be. Wholesale and consumer prices surged higher into 1974–75 and then underwent a secondary rise into the early 1980s. It was not until Paul Volcker became chairman of the Federal Reserve System in 1979 that the authorities were seen as being serious about containing inflation.

This disinflationary attitude was critical to the events that followed. It drove the DJIA into a bubble peak in summer 1987, and this peak was – unsurprisingly – followed by a genuine crash. Bubbles are based on a collective recognition of the validity of real change, but the problem is that markets initially expect too much. The subsequent crash is usually so severe that it eliminates optimistic expectations. However, one beneficial result is that it also creates spare financial resources for the next advance.

It is very clear that the Life Cycle Hypothesis allows the dimension of **time** to be used as a direct input into investment decisions. A bubble-and-crash identifies the presence of a Transition Cycle. Looking backwards, it is then possible to find the nature and timing of the creative shock and, looking forward, it is possible to anticipate the likely duration of three rhythmic cycles. Indeed, as the life cycle progresses, the timing and implications of all subsequent oscillations become clearer.

The crash within the Transition Cycle is the first energy gap in the overall life cycle. The Transition Cycle is then followed by a Transformation Cycle, which lays down the changes for the evolving era. Finally, the Transformation Cycle is followed by a Termination Cycle, which relies on existing beliefs and ideas. Inevitably, the Termination Cycle is punctuated by a second – and terminal – energy gap. The onset of the energy gap – possibly in 2016, and certainly in 2017 – implies that the authorities no longer regard disinflation as a priority. This helps to explain why equities are continuing to rise. The problem, of course, is that the energy gap is the final one for the whole life cycle that began in 1970. Current developments will therefore have longer-term implications.

# 8

## Lower-Level Life Cycles

### Introduction

L IFE CYCLES INTRODUCE a workable approach to 'time'. Once the life cycle of a specific type of change has begun, major turning points start to become predictable; and, the longer that such a life cycle has been evolving, the more predictable it becomes. However, life cycles are hierarchical in nature, which is one of the reasons why they are difficult to use for short-term timings. Lower-level cycles will be distorted by higher-level cycles. Sometimes, however, lower-level cycles are so pronounced that they cannot be ignored. Once this has been recognised, they can be used with some precision.

This is the case with the rise in the DJIA that has emerged since the March 2009 low. As we saw in the last chapter, that advance belongs to a Termination Cycle. Since such cycles are highly speculative, they generate excesses; and these excesses ultimately ensure that the overall life cycle trips into its second – and final – energy gap. Such gaps are the beginning of the end for the whole life cycle. It therefore has serious implications.

In this chapter, the life cycle used in Chapter 7 will be termed the 'higher-level' cycle. Specifically, the Termination Cycle that started at the 2009 low and that is due to end in early 2023, is a higher-level Termination Cycle. If we can identify lower-level cycles within this Termination Cycle, it should be possible to track the performance of the DJIA into its final energy gap.

### Lower-level life cycles

Figure 8-1 shows the behaviour of the DJIA both during and after the 2007–09 equity bear. In this chart, and those that follow, the left-hand vertical axis relating to the DJIA is shown in arithmetic, rather than logarithmic, form.

Momentum in the DJIA itself is then tracked on the right-hand vertical axis using a six-month rate of change, rather than a five-year rate of change. A faster moving momentum indicator is often more useful in tracking shorter-term behaviour in a market. Overlaid on the DJIA and its momentum are two other indices. The first, shown by a thick black dashed line, is the high-level Termination Cycle itself. The second, shown by the thin grey dashed line, is the lower-level life cycle that was triggered into being by the run-up to, and emergence of, the 2007–09 financial crisis.

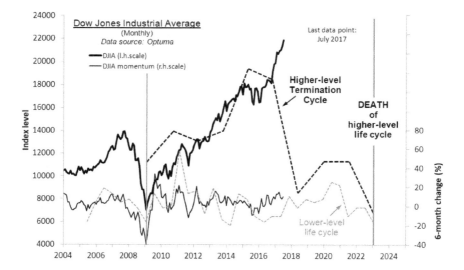

Figure 8-1: The DJIA lower-level life cycle

Figure 8-1 immediately makes clear that there is a directional disparity between the higher-level life cycle and the lower-level cycle. The former started to turn down in mid-2015, which need not create immediate difficulties. A change in direction in the life cycle that is only modest allows for other factors to come into play. As it happened, though, the downturn did suppress the DJIA. The real issue is that the higher-level life cycle moved into an energy gap at the end of 2016, but the market still continued to rise. It seems that, in the first half of 2017, the DJIA has been responding to an advance in its lower-level life cycle. This needs an explanation.

## Higher-level and lower-level life cycles

The starting point is to understand the exact nature of the higher-level energy gap. It does not relate *just* to the DJIA; it is a reflection of broader developments. The higher-level life cycle almost certainly relates to the impact of monetary policy in the context of disinflation. It is, for example, notable that the authorities could not reflate after the 1973–74 collapse in the DJIA because stimulative monetary policies had been the prime cause of inflation – and the authorities knew it. In the case of 2017, therefore, the energy gap means that monetary policy monetary policy is still operating in a deflationary environment. This means that the authorities cannot take the risk of raising interest rates significantly. It also means that inflation will increasingly become a threat.

The other influence is monetary policy itself. As we saw in Chapter 7, US monetary policy has become increasingly bound up with the monetary policies of other nations – particularly with those of continental Europe, the UK, and Japan. Global monetary policy was undoubtedly stimulative in the early part of 2017. This is consistent with the lower-level Transformation Cycle that was then unfolding. Between autumn 2013 and summer 2015, there was a shift away from the beliefs and attitudes that drove the DJIA higher in 2009–13. There was a growing conviction that the US authorities saw a fall in the DJIA as being a threat to the health of the US economy. This automatically implied that the Fed would provide a safety net against another financial crisis.[78] The inference was that the authorities were biased towards reflation and would not tighten monetary policy aggressively.

This meant that, as the lower-level life cycle entered the trend phase of its Transformation Cycle, the DJIA was likely to rally. Inflation expectations were rising, but only modestly, and the global monetary authorities were reflating. This means that problems are unlikely to develop in a major way until the excesses of the trend phase demand a correction.

## The lower-level creative shock

We need to go back to the **start** of the lower-level life cycle to understand what has happened. The 2007–09 crisis was a traumatic event for financial markets, but it remains a matter of opinion as to when the problems related to this trauma actually started. As presented in Figure 8-1, the problems seem to have condensed into an information shock in early 2005. This was when official reflation started to have an impact. Market participants had to **learn** that reflation was becoming permanent.

---

78    This, it has to be added, was the collective belief that preceded the Wall Street Crash.

If we assume that this learning phase started in mid-2005, then it almost certainly ended in spring 2009 at the end of the global financial crisis. Learning periods usually indicate that they are finished when there is an explicit event that reflects the alteration in collective psychology. Occasionally, however, a reversal in the market itself transmits the necessary information. In late 2008, the Fed began a process of aggressive monetary stimulus in the form of buying securities from the market.[79] Furthermore, after March 2009, the DJIA began to recover. Both events were consistent with a change in collective psychology.

In either case, the initial recovery in the DJIA between March and December 2009 was based on a lower-level Transition Cycle. The unusual development at this stage was that the authorities were convinced that reflation – which caused the problem in the first place – was the **solution** to the problem. Hence, although the official purchase of securities was halted in the summer of 2010, such purchases were resumed again when economic activity was found not to be recovering strongly.[80] The DJIA responded accordingly.

## Lower level sub-cycles

Figure 8-2 is a modified version of Figure 8-1. It now shows the lower-level life cycle converted into its momentum format. The diagram therefore shows the unfolding – actual and proposed – of the relevant Transition, Transformation, and Termination Cycles. The lower-level Transition Cycle started in March 2009 and ended – probably – in September 2013; the subsequent Transformation Cycle is due to finish in the first half of 2018; and the Termination Cycle should then finish (together with the whole higher-level life cycle) in late 2022 or early 2023.

There will undoubtedly have to be some flexibility assigned to this profile but, as it stands, there appears to be a close relationship between the higher-level Termination Cycle and the lower-level sub-cycles. We need to look at each of these sub-cycles in turn.

---

[79]   This is euphemistically known as "quantitative easing".
[80]   This represents a complete misunderstanding of what actually was happening. See Chapter 9.

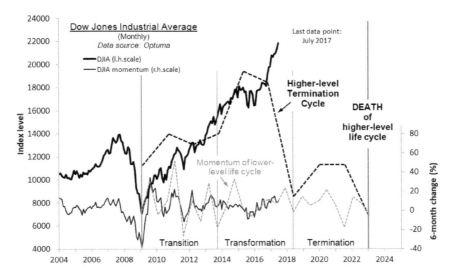

Figure 8-2: Lower-level sub-cycles

## The lower-level Transition Cycle

Figure 8-3 shows the performance of the DJIA and its momentum between early 2008 and late 2013. The legend in the diagram is the same as in the longer charts. The dashed grey line, which tracks the momentum of the lower-level life cycle, here reflects just the shape of the lower-level Transition Cycle.

As is very often the case when a market emerges from a major fall, the presence of a Transition Cycle is very clear in the momentum index. It is, however, unusual in the sense that, after the April–September 2011 fall, downswings in the DJIA were relatively limited. That is, the falls indicated by the Transition Cycle pattern were constrained. Importantly, the same phenomenon occurred after the 1987 equity crash. The similarities between the two periods involved point to the fact that the DJIA was being stimulated by government intervention.

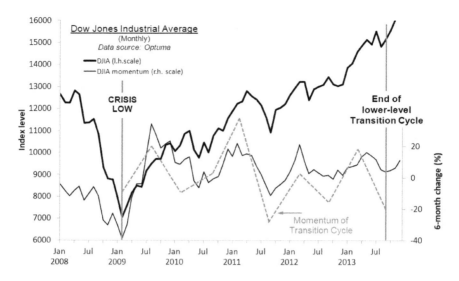

Figure 8-3: The lower-level Transition Cycle

## The lower-level Transformation Cycle

When a Transition Cycle has finished, a market should perform very strongly. The emergence of a lower-level Transformation Cycle is therefore part of the explanation for the strength of the DJIA's advance between autumn 2013 and late 2014. Another element, however, is the fact that the archetypal pattern behind the higher-level Termination Cycle started to turn into its major (highly speculative) uptrend in late 2013. This is very clear in Figure 8-2. At this stage, therefore, the lower- and higher-level life cycles were synchronised.

Figure 8-4 shows the DJIA (the thick black line), the six-month momentum of the DJIA (the thin line), and the archetypal pattern of a Transformation Cycle (the grey dashed line) that began to unfold in the autumn of 2013. For simplicity, the Transformation Cycle is compared directly with the momentum of the DJIA. Nevertheless, the shape of oscillations in the DJIA itself obviously needs to be taken into account as well.

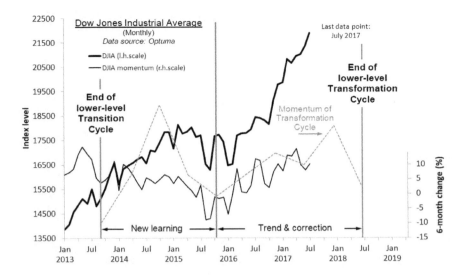

Figure 8-4: The lower-level Transformation Cycle

## New learning in the Transformation Cycle

As argued in Chapter 3, a Transformation Cycle will normally have three main elements: new learning, a trend, and a correction. The learning phase ran from September 2013 to around October 2015. That learning almost certainly involved the Federal Reserve's willingness to support the markets. In June 2013, the DJIA had fallen sharply because Fed Chairman Ben Bernanke had announced that the contemporaneous bout of quantitative easing would be "tapered". In September 2013, the Fed reversed its stance.[81]

By late 2013, therefore, it had become patently clear that the authorities were not prepared to upset market psychology. In other words, their policy target had transmuted from stimulating output to supporting equities. This is why the advance through 2014 and early 2015 was so sustained. Between the start of the lower-level Transformation Cycle in September 2013 and the market peak in February 2015, the DJIA advanced by more than 22%.

The presence of a learning cycle also helps to explain the significant weakness in the DJIA in September 2015 and again in January 2016. The severity of

[81]    On 18 September 2013, the Fed announced that it would suspend further tapering and would not increase official interest rates. Tapering of the official purchases of bonds was restarted in January 2014 and was stopped altogether in late October 2014.

these falls highlighted the importance to collective psychology of what was happening. They straddled the scheduled end of the learning phase, and tested the authorities' commitment to stability.[82] The Fed, in its September 2015 statement, accordingly reaffirmed its commitment to "accommodative monetary conditions".[83]

## The trend

After this learning period was over, the DJIA was able to enter the trend phase of its lower-level life cycle. This trend was responsible for the dynamism of the DJIA's rise after January 2016, and Figure 8-4 suggests that this upswing should last until late 2017. It is important to note, however, that the **new ideas** on which the DJIA's rise was based merely reflected an intensification of the belief that monetary policy would remain supportive. Very little account appears to have been taken of the message from the higher-level life cycle that the link between monetary policy and economic activity was breaking down.

This means, of course, that the DJIA will become increasingly vulnerable to profit-taking as the advance continues. In early 2017, the DJIA had to negotiate a period of sluggishness – expressed primarily in momentum – prior to its final advance. But the main test still lies ahead: a correction is due to start in late 2017, and it should persist into mid-2018. Figure 8-2 suggests that this correction will combine neatly with the closing stages of the higher-level energy gap that is still unfolding. Hence, a 'technical' correction will run the risk of locking into 'fundamental' concerns about the future. It will not be an easy time.

## The lower-level Termination Cycle

It is important to emphasise that the lower-level Termination Cycle that is scheduled to start in mid-2018 will be overlaid on – and will therefore be integrated with – the end phase of the higher-level Termination Cycle that began in March 2009. Because both phases lie in the future, we can only review them in their schematic form. This situation is shown in Figure 8-5. The aftermath of the higher-level energy gap is shown by the black dashed line, and the lower-level Termination Cycle is shown by the grey dashed line.

There are a number of important points. The first is that, from a low in mid-2018, the lower-level Termination Cycle allows a rally into mid-2020. In principle,

---

[82]   Between 19 May and 24 August 2015, the DJIA fell by over 16%. This fall was a 38.2% retracement of the major upswing between October 2011 and May 2015. Prior to that, the October 2011 low was formed at a 38.2% retracement of the recovery from March 2009 to April 2011. The 38.2% retracement boundary is/was highly significant. See Appendix II.

[83]   www.federalreserve.gov/newsevents/pressreleases/monetary20150917a.htm.

there should be a correction in the first part of 2019, but the higher-level life cycle will be in an up-phase over more or less the same period. Consequently, the outcome is indeterminate. However, if we use the lower-level Termination Cycle as a guide, the natural end of the bull advance that started in March 2009 should occur sometime around June 2020.

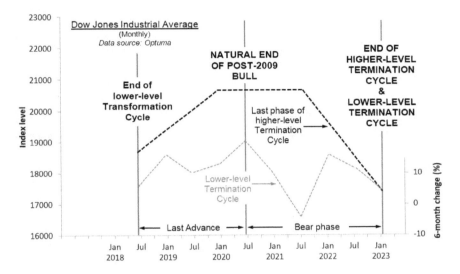

Figure 8-5: The lower-level Termination Cycle

Whether or not the DJIA can actually reach this date at a new all-time high can only be a matter of conjecture. We have already seen that a deep correction is due between late 2017 and mid-2018, but we cannot yet know either how far the DJIA will fall over that period or whether that fall will trigger a strategic reversal signal.[84] What we can guess, however, is that the bear phase between mid-2020 and early 2023 will be severe. It will involve an energy gap in the lower-level Termination Cycle; it will involve the death phase of the higher-level Termination Cycle; and it will undoubtedly involve a recognition of inflation pressures in the system.

---

84    See Appendix II.

# Conclusion

This chapter has tracked the after-effects of the 2007–09 global financial crisis through the lens of what has been termed a 'lower-level' life cycle. The evidence is that, between 2009 and 2015, this lower-level cycle evolved in a close relationship with the higher-level cycle. However, the two cycles have since parted company: the higher-level cycle is in its second energy gap, but the lower-level cycle is in the rising stage of its Transformation Cycle. The energy gap in the higher-level cycle is almost certainly indicating that US monetary policy is still operating in an environment of weak inflation. Nevertheless, the problems may not become apparent until late 2017/early 2018, when the lower-level Transformation Cycle re-synchronises with the higher-level energy gap.

In principle, the subsequent recovery through late 2018 and into 2020 could be strong because the higher- and lower-level life cycles are synchronised. However, the lower-level cycle will at that stage be in its Termination Cycle. This, by nature, will be highly speculative, and we can only guess at the excesses that this may cause. What we can be more certain about, however, is that the terminal energy gap in the lower-level cycle – which is due to become apparent in the second half of 2020 – will synchronise with the 'death' phase of the higher-level cycle. This suggests that the period 2020–23 will be extremely difficult.

# 9

# The 36-Year Cycle In Industrial Production

## Introduction

IN CHAPTER 3, I showed how a life cycle can be converted into oscillations that are both patterned and rhythmic. In Chapter 8, I then used such a transformation to track and interpret progress in the DJIA since 2009. The secret is to translate the life cycle into a momentum series, using a one-period change. To some extent, it doesn't matter whether we use the life cycle itself or its momentum to track an index; where one exists, so does the other. Nevertheless, momentum is often more useful in tracking rhythmic cycles. In addition, momentum can be better applied to some series rather than to others. It is particularly useful where the original series is naturally presented in terms of rates of change.

Life cycle momentum has three characteristics that are useful for analysing oscillations in US industrial production. Firstly, each end-of-cycle energy gap can generate a new sequence of cycles. The energy gap therefore operates as a shock in its own right.[85] Secondly, each of the sub-cycles oscillates with a constant periodicity. This allows us to identify fixed-term cycles in the data series. Finally, of course, each of the evolutionary sub-cycles contains a potential interruption. This enables us accurately to anticipate those periodic weaknesses in economic growth that are a cause for political concern.

---

[85]   Theoretically, of course, the cause of the energy gap may come from outside the immediate system being analysed. Nevertheless, the resulting shock can be treated as being endogenous.

# A look at the data

The Federal Reserve Bank of St Louis makes available each month an index of US industrial production. The index runs from January 1919, is currently set to 2012=100, and is seasonally adjusted.[86] The raw index is as shown in Figure 9-1. The 12-month percentage change in that index is shown in Figure 9-2. It is immediately clear that the oscillations were very large at the beginning of the period. The momentum series clearly picks out the low of 1921 and, more significantly, the low of 1932. It also picks out the lows of 1938 and 1946. It is usual to consider the weakness of 1921 and 1946 as being post-war adjustments, and then categorise the troughs of 1932 and 1938 as belonging to the Great Depression.

Figure 9-1: Index of US industrial production since 1919

It is also clear from the momentum chart that the oscillations in output have lessened in recent years. There were, however, pronounced lows in 1974 and 2009. The former is usually attributed to the **response to inflation**; the latter is inevitably described as a **cause of deflation**. This asymmetry hints at the presence of forces that are not recognised by conventional analysis. Neo-

---

[86] Board of Governors of the Federal Reserve System (US), Industrial Production Index [INDPRO], retrieved from Federal Reserve Bank of St. Louis: https://fred.stlouisfed.org/series/INDPRO, April 1, 2017.

Keynesian theory assumes that wise governments can offset the failings of the imprudent private sector. However, taken together, the experiences of 1974 and 2009 suggest that this is not true. In fact, the evidence suggests instead that government intervention may ultimately be de-stabilising.

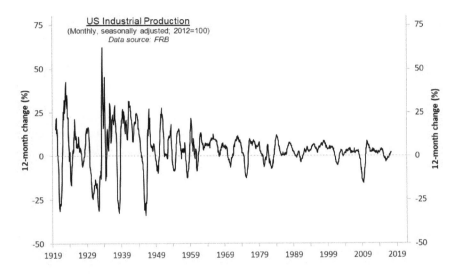

Figure 9-2: Momentum of US industrial production

It is usual for economists to focus, not on the **level** of industrial production, but on the **rates of change** in the level of industrial production. This, after all, is the definition of 'growth'. It is, however, quite noticeable from Figure 9-1, that the buoyancy of industrial production has subsided since 2000. In fact, it has broken down through its post-war uptrend. There are a number of reasons that can be given for this, especially: (i) the switch from manufacturing to services; (ii) the switch from savings to debt; and (iii) the switch away from wealth creation towards wealth redistribution. All of these explanations are correct – not least because they are arising together. But what if they only identify symptoms of deeper-running forces? What if the shift in general attitudes reflects the working of an evolutionary process?

# Interruptions to long-term growth

Figure 9-2 shows that the last significant trough in industrial production occurred in 2009. Prior to that there was a deep low in 1975. This means that there was a 34-year gap between the two events. Using this number as a guide, we can look back and see if there was something similar in 1941. In fact, there was a major low in 1938. This implies an average gap of 35½ years.[87] If we then go back 35½ years, was there a low in or around 1902?

Unfortunately, data from the Federal Reserve Bank of St Louis do not go back that far. Other economists, however, indicate a recession low in 1900 and then a deeper one in 1904. The National Bureau of Economic Research, for example, suggests that an 18-month contraction ended in late 1900 and that a 23-month contraction ended in 1904. I suspect that the latter date is the one to use. It was deeper than its immediate predecessor and was associated with a major fall in equities that became known as a 'rich man's panic'.[88] In any case, the figures suggest that the average duration between energy gap lows is between 35 and 36 years.[89]

# 36-year economic lows

The finding of a sequence of economic lows that are close to being 36 years apart is significant. First, the number 36 belongs to an important number set that was almost certainly used by William Gann. Details of this number set are included in Appendix I. Second, the periodicity between the economic lows of 1904, 1938, 1975, and 2009 is more or less constant. This is not the same thing as saying that the periodicity is always precise. Nor does it mean that there aren't other important lows. But it does mean that some form of organised process may be involved. And, third, the economic slowdowns of 1937–38, 1973–75, and 2007–09 were sufficiently severe to have had longer-term consequences. This suggests very strongly that the slowdowns may be energy gaps within Termination Cycles. If so, it should be possible to work backwards, and locate the momentum peaks of the preceding Transition Cycles.

# Transition Cycle peaks

The original life cycle shown in Chapter 1 indicates that the peak of a Transition Cycle occurs about one-third of the way into the whole of a life cycle, albeit

---

[87]   That is, (2009–1938) / 2 = 35.5.
[88]   These conclusions are consistent with the findings presented in Chapter 10.
[89]   That is, (2009–1904) / 2 = 35, or (2009–1900) / 2 = 36.33.

with some variability.⁹⁰ There is, however, a complication. This is that industrial production life cycles **overlap** each other, such that the beginnings of each new life cycle are embedded in the endings of an old one. Every new learning phase will include, but transcend, the terminal shock from the previous life cycle. Consequently, the actual life cycle will be longer than the 36 years indicated by the time elapse between energy gaps.

## The overlap

In practical terms, therefore, the duration of each life cycle has to be adjusted for an overlap. The best way of showing this is to use an example. In this case, we shall use the Termination Cycle within the 1942–78 life cycle, and the learning phase at the beginning of the 1978–2012/13 life cycle.⁹¹ Figure 9-3 accordingly shows three series: the 12-month percentage change in US industrial production (heavy black line); the archetypal pattern of the old life cycle (dashed grey line); and the archetypal pattern of the new life cycle (dashed black line).

The diagram indicates a close correlation between the schematic pathways for the old and new cycles. In reality, however, the correlation is unlikely to be so precise. One difficulty is that the start and end points of each life cycle inevitably contain some flexibility. In addition, the energy involved in the changeover is likely to oscillate significantly, as the system tries to adjust to changing circumstances. One of the obvious changes is that the new cycle will have to incorporate a change in attitudes, so that genuine evolution can begin. These characteristics are very difficult to track using a constant-duration momentum index.

90   The peak number of pages in *Tunnel* is in Chapter 12. If we compare this with all 36 chapters, the peak is 34% of the way along; if we compare it with the 35 chapters that trace out the life cycle pattern, the peak is 33% of the way through the pattern. Moreover, if Chapter 1 of *Tunnel* is treated as 0% and Chapter 35 is 100%, then the 12th chapter occurs at 32% of the way through the pattern.

91   There is some uncertainty about the end date of this cycle. European economies clearly show end dates of late 2012. In the US, however, the 12-month change in output didn't stop falling until mid-2013. An end-date of late 2012 means that the duration of the Termination Cycle equates with the duration of the prior Transition and Transformation Cycles. However, an end-date of mid-2013 makes the duration of the whole cycle closer than otherwise to 36 years.

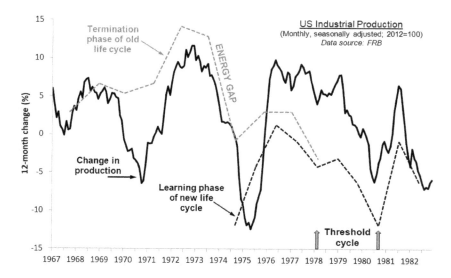

Figure 9-3: The overlap between cycles

## The learning phase

In Figure 9-3, the energy gap of the old life cycle ended in 1974, but the recession continued into early 1975. In the diagram, this mismatch is associated with a learning phase – specifically that runaway inflation had appalling consequences and had to be contained. The aftermath of the energy gap in the old life cycle therefore began to integrate with the realisation that the authorities could be forced to adjust their policies. However – and this is very important – recognising that policies will probably change is not the same thing as policies actually changing. Such measures involve the psychological commitment to transformation, and then the implementation of the necessary adjustments. Neither is easy, and both take time. This is why the Threshold Cycle is so important.

## The Threshold Cycle

The recognition that attitudes need to change is intimately related to the Threshold Cycle. This cycle, which is a doorway into the new era, occurs at the end of the learning phase of a new life cycle. In the context of industrial production, the Threshold Cycle usually takes the form of a very simple inventory cycle: there is an initial rise followed by a more prolonged fall. Somewhat confusingly for politicians and conventional economists, the cycle will be heavily influenced by the end-of cycle energy gap that has immediately preceded it. It is therefore highly unlikely to involve heavy capital expenditure.

The average duration of a Threshold Cycle is 3¼ to 3½ years, although there can be some significant variability. In practice, the duration has been as little as two years or as long as five. The important point is that the end of the Threshold Cycle is signalled when there is an explicit change in mood. The signal may just take the form of an economic upswing; however, it is much more likely to be associated with an observable socio-political adjustment. These include events such as a change in political leadership or in economic policy.[92] Such events may pre-date, coincide with, or post-date, an economic upswing.

## From start to finish

The implication is that the 36-year time elapse between end-of-cycle energy gaps is consistent with longer, but overlapping life cycles. In fact, looked at separately, each life cycle can have a duration of between 38 and 43 years. In practice, however, we will be measuring the duration between the start of a Threshold Cycle and the end of the later Termination Cycle. This is actually the same calculation as measuring the duration between the end of one life cycle and the end of the next one. In either case, the time elapse involved will be about 36 years. But, of course, some leeway has to be applied to this figure.

## From the high to low

In *Tunnel*, the peak of a Transition Cycle occurred about one-third of the way through a whole life cycle. If the latter's length is between 38 and 43 years, this means that the Transition Cycle peak will impact somewhere between 25 years and 29 years after the life cycle starts. However, this timing may not always be obvious if the events surrounding the start of the life cycle are traumatic. The easiest solution, therefore, is to use the Threshold Cycle (which should be more obvious) as the starting point. In this case, we can anticipate the Transition Cycle peak in either of two ways. Firstly, the Transition Cycle peak will occur six to nine years after the Threshold Cycle begins. Or, secondly, the Transition Cycle peak will impact four to five years after the Threshold Cycle ends. Very often, the latter is the more useful because the duration of the Threshold Cycle is so variable.

---

92    In the newly-emerging era, the Threshold Cycle has been terminated by the election in 2016 of an outsider – i.e., Donald Trump – to the office of president of the USA.

## Socio-economic eras

The general outcome is as shown in Figure 9-4, which covers changes in US industrial production since 1919. The Termination Cycle lows of 1938, 1975, and 2009 are clearly identified, as are the Transition Cycle highs of 1950 and 1984. The grey shaded areas represent the Threshold Cycles: 1942–46, 1978–80, and 2012/13–16. Importantly, once these Threshold Cycles are included in calculating the length of a cycle, we can identify two great economic cycles. These cycles had quite profound social consequences, and so they can be denoted as 'socio-economic eras'. The first is 1942–78, and is 36 years in length; the second era is 1978–2012/13, and is 34–35 years in length.

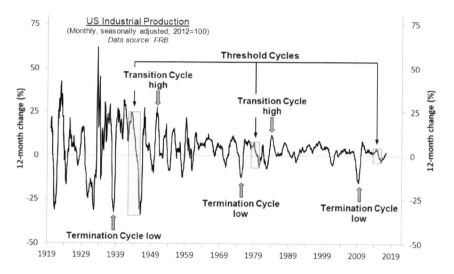

Figure 9-4: Socio-economic eras

## The 1942–78 era

These are extraordinary conclusions in their own right, especially considering that economic activity is supposed to be dependent only on independent private and public-sector decision-making. However, there is more. A closer inspection of Figure 9-4 reveals that each of the two eras evolves in a very similar way. We can therefore look at each of them as independent entities and see to what extent they reflect the ideal life cycle pattern.

Figure 9-5 shows the first socio-economic era. The heavy line shows the 12-month percentage change in industrial production; the dashed line shows the momentum of the life cycle; and the diagram is divided in such a way as to show the underlying cyclical oscillations. Figure 9-5 accordingly starts with a Threshold Cycle (1942–46), and then proceeds through three oscillations of equal duration: the Transition Cycle (1946–56); the Transformation Cycle (1956–67); and the Termination Cycle (1967–1978). The whole pattern takes 36 years to complete: the Threshold Cycle takes about four years (and the schematic has been adjusted to take account of this); and each of the subsequent sub-cycles takes just over 10½ years.

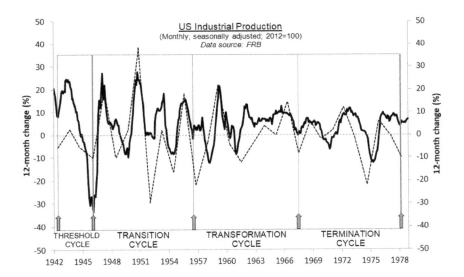

Figure 9-5: The 1942–1978 era

## 1942–78: A brief history

In terms of Figure 9-5, the Threshold Cycle covered the period when the US was involved in WWII. America entered the war after the Japanese attack on Pearl Harbour in December 1941, and finally ended the war with the dropping of atom bombs on Japan in August 1945. The imminent end of the cycle was undoubtedly marked by the Japanese surrender. The actual low of the cycle was then registered by industrial production in February 1946.

The Transition Cycle, which started in 1946, was subject to significant oscillations. There was an initial three-phase surge into a peak in 1950. However, the Korean War started in June 1950, and, as a result, the next significant move was an energy gap. It was this energy gap that ensured that the collective readjustment in the subsequent Transformation Cycle included an ongoing confrontation with Communism. The war in Korea ended in 1953; the transition phase of evolution ended in 1956.

The Transformation Cycle started in 1956. This cycle is particularly important. It includes the halfway point of the whole life cycle, it involves a period of evolutionary learning, and it incorporates new attitudes and ideas about the economy. This would have been the period when official policy included resistance to Communism, when government became more proactive in managing economic expectations, and when the consumer revolution got underway. Eventually, expectations ran too far ahead of reality. There was therefore a recession in 1966–67. However, reflecting the intrinsic strength of the economy during this period, most analysts see the recession as being more of a contraction in growth rather than a reflection of economic weakness. The transformation phase ended in 1967.

The Termination Cycle started in 1967. By this stage, the Cold War with the Soviet bloc was in full swing, and the US had become involved in a war in Vietnam. As the period progressed, the authorities became increasingly willing to finance their military needs by printing money. The US economy was therefore becoming vulnerable to shocks. There was a deep recession between 1969 and 1970, and the authorities responded with a Keynesian stimulus. This stimulus was initially successful, but it also unleashed the forces of inflation onto the economy. Between 1973 and 1975, industrial production encountered an energy gap. This gap started the ending process for the whole cycle. The cycle ended in 1978.

# The 1978–2012/13 era

Figure 9-6 shows the second socio-economic era to have evolved in the period after WWII. The heavy line shows the 12-month percentage change in industrial production; the dashed line shows the momentum of the life cycle; and the diagram is divided in such a way as to show the underlying cyclical oscillations. Figure 9-6 accordingly starts with a Threshold Cycle (1978–80), and then proceeds through three oscillations of equal duration: the Transition Cycle (1980–91); the Transformation Cycle (1991–2001); and the Termination Cycle (2001–2012/13). The whole pattern takes 34–35 years to complete: the Threshold Cycle takes just two years (and the schematic has been adjusted to take account of this); and each of the subsequent sub-cycles takes about 11 years.

## 1978–2012/13: A brief history

The Threshold Cycle started in early 1978, and turned out to be shorter than usual. It evolved during a highly inflationary period for the US economy, and the signal that it was finishing (and that uncontrollable inflation was coming to an end) was the selection of Paul Volcker as chairman of the Federal Reserve System. Mr Volcker arrived at the Fed in August 1979, and was committed to an anti-inflation programme. The low of the Threshold Cycle occurred in July 1980.

The Transition Cycle that then started in July 1980 was particularly volatile in its early stages because the authorities were still struggling to control inflation. There was a particularly deep recession in 1982. However, it was not until the energy gap materialised after 1984 that the system started genuinely to adjust to a disinflationary environment. Even then the destruction was not completed until after the slump of 1990–91 had ended. The Transition Cycle finished in 1991.

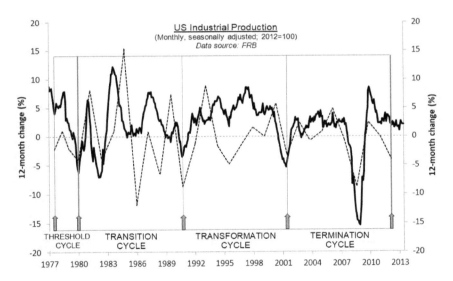

Figure 9-6: The 1978–2012/13 era

The Transformation Cycle accordingly started in 1991. The learning stage of the cycle incorporated the central idea that the government could – and would – control inflation. This allowed the economy to enter a particularly strong period. Whereas the 1956–67 cycle embraced a consumer revolution, the 1991–2001 cycle embraced a technological revolution. The 1990s therefore oversaw the growth of digital technology, the widening use of computers and mobile phones, and the beginnings of social networking. In 2000, however, there was a crash in technology shares, which warned that the period was coming to an end. There was a very deep recession in 2000–01. The cycle ended in 2001.

The Termination Cycle started as its predecessor finished. Termination Cycles do not normally involve a major insertion of new ideas into an evolving system. They are periods of trial and error: the trial consists of taking known ideas and methodologies to their limits; the error is the resulting excesses. These excesses generate an end-of-cycle energy gap. In this case, there was a very deep recession in 2008–09 – probably the worst since the Great Depression of the 1930s. The authorities responded by applying a Keynesian stimulus to the economy; and it didn't work. As was indicated in Figure 9-1, industrial production broke down through its long-term uptrend. The Termination Cycle should then have ended in late 2012. However, ongoing problems suppressed output until mid-2013.

## Convergences and divergences

Despite the obvious – and extraordinary – correspondences between fluctuations in industrial production and oscillations in the archetypal life cycle patterns, there are still some differences. One relates to the duration of the Threshold Cycle; another is the potential for differences between the theoretical and actual finishing dates of the Transition, Transformation, and Termination Cycles; and the final difference is the timing of the terminal energy gap. It is important, therefore to emphasise that, throughout the unfolding of a life cycle, the inherent patterns **never** disappear. They remain in action throughout every 36-year cycle.

Where divergences do appear, they are caused by the dynamics of the underlying behaviour. Collective perceptions are relatively inflexible at the best of times. So, on this basis alone, it is amazing that they can align themselves so clearly with a predetermined configuration. But collective behaviour will have to respond to contemporaneous influences and to rapidly shifting energies. Actual inflexion points may therefore be reached prior to, at, or after the precise moment indicated by the blueprint. Nevertheless, the differences are small in the context of a major life cycle. Even the delay in the arrival of a second energy gap at the end of the 1942–78 cycle amounted to only a year. The important point, however, is that the gap still happened.

## Predictive capabilities

The Life Cycle Hypothesis, with its unchanging patterns, provides a portal into an accurate prediction for industrial output – not in the sense of decimal point forecasts, but in the much more important sense of the timing of important events, the direction of change, and the power behind any movement. One method, which we shall address in the next chapter, is to average the previous cycles and track current developments against that average. The other is to track current developments just against the schematic pattern of the life cycle itself.

Figure 9-7 shows the situation for the US industrial production as at June 2017. The heavy line shows the 12-month percentage change in the Federal Reserve Board's (FRB's) official index; the dashed line is the schematic representation of life cycle momentum. Until we know for certain whether the previous life cycle ended in late 2012 or mid-2013, any analysis has to allow for some degree of flexibility in the timing.

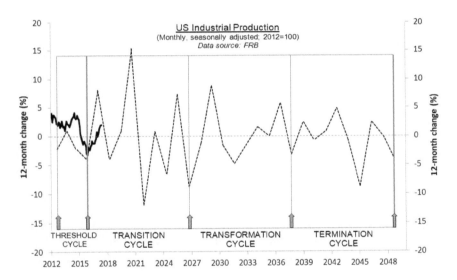

Figure 9-7: The newly-evolving era

## The Threshold Cycle for the new era

It is already apparent that an old life cycle began its ending process, and that a new life cycle was triggered into being, by the trauma of the 2007–09 financial collapse. The actual evidence of that changeover came with the end of the Threshold Cycle in December 2015 and with the election in November 2016 of Donald Trump as US president. The former was followed by a recovery in the momentum of production, which signalled a change in mood; the latter indicated that a large percentage of the electorate were willing to accept an unconventional president, which confirmed that a change in mood had taken place.

If we assume that the terminal juncture of the old life cycle occurred in late 2012, then the Threshold Cycle into the new era spanned about 3¼ years. This conforms to the historical average for an ordinary business cycle. It also means that the whole life cycle lasted for 34⅔ years, which is a little shorter than might have been expected. If, on the other hand, the old life cycle ended in mid-2013, the Threshold Cycle will have lasted for only 2½ years. However, the whole life cycle will then have lasted for 35⅓ years, which is close to the historical average for a socio-economic era.

## Into the Transition Cycle

In either case, once the Threshold Cycle ends, then a disruptive Transition Cycle begins. This means that the upswing in the momentum of production since December 2015 has signalled the start of such a cycle. It is important to note, however, that this may not be a great cause for celebration. The initial upswing in a Transition Cycle is inevitably followed by a renewed slowdown. The equivalent stages in 1947–49 and 1981–82 produced serious weakness. Figure 9-7 therefore allows for economic weakness into 2018–19.

Once this slowdown has finished, the Transition Cycle pattern predicts a more dynamic recovery into a significant peak in 2020. In this sense, the pick-up in momentum since December 2015 is anticipating better times. The problem, however, is that the dynamism of the recovery between 2018–19 and 2020 is likely to be more quantitative than qualitative. And it will be followed by an energy gap. This gap, which will start in 2021 and may continue into 2022, will activate the first socio-economic mutation within the new era. Its specific task will be to trigger the unwinding of any excesses. It will therefore target any excesses that still remain from before the 2007–09 financial crisis, and it will target all related overindulgences since that crisis. It is likely to be devastating.

We cannot yet know what will cause these swings, but we can know that they are likely. These are not the sort of predictions that can be found in the more conventional linear economic models.

## Conclusion

This chapter has applied the Life Cycle Hypothesis to fluctuations in industrial production since WWII. The period was easily separated into two socio-economic eras of around 36 years each: 1942–78 and 1978–2012/13. Both eras could then be divided into four phases: a two- to four-year Threshold Cycle;

a 10- to 11-year Transition Cycle; a 10- to 11-year Transformation Cycle; and a 10- to 11-year Termination Cycle.

The overall correlations between the predicted fluctuations and actual oscillations were stunning. In both eras, the Threshold Cycle ended with an observable event that signalled a change of mood. In both eras, the momentum of production then unfolded exactly as predicted by the Life Cycle Hypothesis: the Transition Cycle produced a strong three-wave advance followed by an energy gap; the Transformation Cycle oversaw a period of new ideas and significant innovation; and, finally, the Termination Cycle generated significant excesses, which then spawned a major energy gap.[93]

Apart from some minor differences, therefore, the momentum of industrial production follows a very specific predetermined pattern – and does so with a high degree of accuracy. This has far-reaching implications for policy-making and for economic theory. Given the grip that the politics of wealth redistribution currently exert in Western democracies, an immediate paradigm shift is highly unlikely. But it is no accident that political intervention intensified prior to the crises of 1937–38, 1973–75 and 2007–09. And it is no accident that official attempts to deal with the after-effects of the first two of those catastrophes resulted in periods of adjustment that were both volatile and lengthy. It is unlikely that the recovery from the 2007–09 disaster will escape the same fate.

93    It is worth noting here that the 1937–38 implosion classifies as a final energy gap.

# *10*

## The Era Of The Great Depression

### Introduction

THE LIFE CYCLE pattern makes very clear that genuine growth is impossible without periods of rest. Modern economic theory assumes, however, that the public sector can offset these rest periods, and make recessions unnecessary. This assumption dates from the extraordinary economic collapse of the 1930s, which convinced economic theorists and politicians that the public sector should be more proactive in offsetting the alleged mistakes of the private sector. In this chapter we shall take a closer look at quantitative fluctuations in business activity during the Great Depression and see to what extent they were different from those experienced after WWII. This should enable us to draw practical conclusions about whether government policy can be sufficiently independent to limit the impact of natural recessions.

### The index of business activity

The Life Cycle Hypothesis relies on the availability of long time series. With respect to business activity, there are currently two sources: the Board of Governors of the Federal Reserve System (FRB), and the National Bureau of Economic Research (NBER). The data from FRB is monthly, but goes back only until 1919, while the data that can be mined from the NBER goes back to the late 18th century, but is only available on an annual basis.

Fortunately, another source is available. A monthly index of US business activity dating from 1790 was calculated by Ameritrust until 1988. More recently, the index has been maintained by Bill Sarubbi at **Cycles Research**. Prior to 1919, the data consists of 20 relevant time series that have been made compatible and concatenated together; after 1919, the official FRB data have been used. Importantly, all the data have been adjusted so that the effects of population growth have been eliminated. Researchers may be able to argue about the validity of specific elements of the earlier data, but the significant feature of the whole series is that it has a very long history. In particular, it will undoubtedly show the correct direction of the momentum in overall business activity.

The life cycle relevant to the Great Depression lasted from 1908 to 1942. In principle, we ought to be able to establish any common features between that life cycle and those that preceded and followed it. In order to make the necessary comparisons, we need to use an index that covers all time periods. Consequently, we first need to apply the Business Activity Index, rather than industrial production, to the two life cycles that unfolded after 1942 – namely, that of 1942–1978 and that of 1978–2012/13. Once this has been done, we can average together the two socio-economic life cycles that were analysed in Chapter 9. The resulting average should emphasize the relationship that has existed since WWII between actual collective behaviour and the archetypal life cycle.

## Standardising the data

Before calculating such an average, however, it is necessary to make an important adjustment. Quite obviously, the duration of each specific era can differ slightly from the duration of the others. For example, the life cycle that incorporated the Great Depression (1908–1942) lasted for 34 years, the first post-war life cycle (1942–1978) lasted for 36 years, and the most recent life cycle (1978–2012/13) lasted for 34–35 years. Obviously, the life cycles that preceded that of 1908–42 can also be of different lengths. We therefore need to stretch the length of the shorter cycles mathematically so that they match the duration of the longest one.

The method chosen has been to break each life cycle down into its Threshold Cycle and its momentum-orientated sub-cycles – i.e., a Transition Cycle, a Transformation Cycle, and a Termination Cycle – and treat the duration of each of these sub-cycles as representing a length of 100%. It is then possible mathematically to stretch each set of sub-cycles so that they become equal to each other. Then a percentage movement from the beginning of a sub-cycle to any particular point becomes directly comparable with the same percentage movement in an equivalent sub-cycle. For the record, the longest sub-cycle, to which all Transition, Transformation, and Termination Cycles have been adjusted, is the 144-month Transformation Cycle of October 1884 to October 1896. This is the cycle that incorporated the longest economic depression prior to that of the 1930s.

## Post-war activity

The average profile of the two life cycles that evolved after 1942 – that is, between 1942 and 1978 and between 1978 and 2012/13 – is shown in Figure 10-1. The thick line tracks the average behaviour of business activity over the two periods; the dashed line represents the expected momentum of a normal life cycle. It is no small matter that the shape of the average Threshold Cycle is as expected, that the energy gaps in the average Transition and Terminal Cycles occur on time, and that the final downswings of the average Transition, Transformation, and Termination Cycles occur exactly as predicted.

The only significant point of divergence between theory and practice occurs at the mid-point between the original initiating shock and the end of the life cycle. This is where the shape of the life cycle will naturally come into potential conflict with its underlying momentum. It is this divergence that allows the Transformation Cycle to incorporate any contemporaneous pressures that spill over from the Transition Cycle. In this case, industrial production and business activity were biased downwards during the recession of 1957–58.

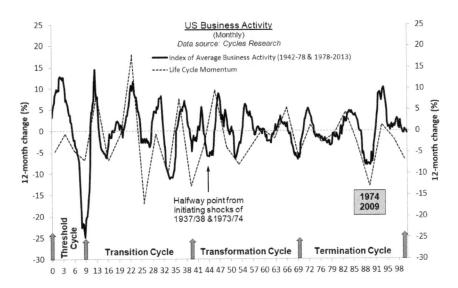

Figure 10-1: The average life cycle after WWII

# The Great Depression

We can now look more closely at business activity during the Great Depression itself. We can then compare its patterns of behaviour to those of other life cycles. Once this has been done, it should be clear whether or not the Great Depression was truly a random phenomenon. Figure 10-2 accordingly covers the 34-year period that incorporated the Great Depression. The period started in May 1908, which was after the financial panic of 1907 had ended, but before the Federal Reserve System was established.[94] The period ended in June 1942, which was six months after the US entered WWII, following the Japanese attack on Pearl Harbour, but a little less than six months before the US joined Britain in invading French North Africa. The fluctuations in business activity are shown as the heavy line; the profile of life cycle momentum is shown as a dashed line. For clarity, the nature of each of the sub-cycles is identified along the lower horizontal axis.

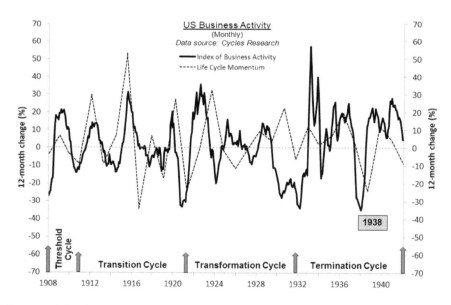

Figure 10-2: The era of the Great Depression

---

[94] It is likely that the 1907 panic was one of the primary driving forces behind the establishment of the Federal Reserve System.

It is clear that business activity oscillated significantly over the period. It is also quite clear that turning points in activity did not synchronise with turning points in expected behaviour. In particular, the Transformation Cycle started earlier and ended later than might have been expected. Nevertheless, business oscillations followed the intrinsic pattern of the life cycle very closely. The Threshold Cycle consisted of a recovery and then contraction, and lasted from spring 1908 to winter 1910/11. The Transition Cycle consisted of a three-wave advance into a peak during WWI, an energy gap, a three-phase recovery, and then a sharp contraction. It lasted from winter 1910/11 until spring/summer 1921. The Transformation Cycle consisted of a sharp initial recovery, a deep retrenchment, a three-phase recovery, and then a final mega-contraction. It extended from spring/summer 1921 until summer 1932. Finally, the Termination Cycle underwent a three-wave advance into excess, an unexpected contraction in 1937/38, and a period of stabilisation. It started in summer 1932 and ended in summer 1942.

If we ignore for the moment the weakness in business activity between 1930 and 1932, it is arguable that the problem was not so much randomness as periodicity. Specifically, the pattern of business activity during the Transformation Cycle adopted a longer time frame than might have been anticipated from the expected pattern. As we shall see below, once the duration of the sub-cycles over the era of the Great Depression are equalised with those that occurred after 1942, the patterns synchronise with those derived from the Life Cycle Hypothesis.

## The Depression-era life cycle

The implication is that business oscillations during the Great Depression were not as random as is often projected. The recession of 1920–21 impacted at the end of the Transition Cycle; the 1929 slowdown started on time, towards the end of the Transformation Cycle; and the sudden economic collapse in 1937–38 materialised in the energy gap of the Termination Cycle. On this basis, the extended fall in business activity between late 1929 and mid-1932 suggests that other forces were at work. These conclusions are, in themselves, revealing. But there is something else: the position of each of the individual recessions within the overall life cycle, together with any obvious distortions away from the cycle's natural pathway, reveals that evolutionary forces were involved.

The first major recession in the sequence – that of 1920–21 – was the outcome of two decisions. First, the US government attempted after WWI to rebalance the public sector budget by cutting spending. Second, the Federal Reserve raised interest rates in order to reverse an outflow of gold. The outcome was a deflationary recession.

Importantly, though, the government also implemented significant tax cuts. The inherent switch from the public to the private sectors accounted for the subsequent economic recovery between March 1921 and December 1922, and then helped to reinforce the social revolution of the Roaring Twenties. It is a significant fact that the policy of **laissez-faire**, and a surge in innovation, persisted throughout the main part of the 1921–32 Transformation Cycle.[95]

The economic contraction that ended the optimism of the 1920s – i.e., the slump of 1929–32 – started earlier than the life cycle pattern would have predicted. One way of looking at this is to argue that, although the shape of the Transformation Cycle was essentially as predicted by the life cycle pattern, a possible recovery between late 1929 and early 1931 was negated by the influence of something unusual. Business activity fell sharply in late 1929, and then kept falling well into 1932.

## A mistake?

Despite being established in December 1913 in order to provide some stability to the banking system, the Federal Reserve allowed the monetary aggregates to contract sharply between 1929 and 1932. It is, of course, arguable that this was entirely consistent with the philosophy of **laissez-faire**, which (among other things) meant that moral jeopardy should be allowed to work through the system. Nevertheless, there is a crucial difference between individual liability and collective stability. This mismatch was not recognised by the authorities, and the supply of credit dropped dramatically. Such a major shock to the economy was very difficult to accommodate, and business activity collapsed. The Great Depression, in other words, was associated with a fatal misunderstanding.[96]

## The 1937–38 energy gap

This analysis provides an interesting background for the final major contraction in the 1908–42 life cycle – the slump of 1937–38. At the time it came as a surprise, and now it tends to be subsumed into the whole phenomenon of the Great Depression. However, the 1937–38 contraction was not a random event. It certainly had a cause in the form of a major contraction in the monetary aggregates; but it was always likely to happen. A functioning life cycle needs just such a shock both to bring its own internal evolutionary processes to an end, and to activate the processes that are appropriate for the subsequent era.

---

[95] The energy of the Transformation Cycle helps to explain why innovation continued to expand during the depression of the 1930s. The life cycle in innovation is covered in more detail in Chapter 14.

[96] This leaves open the question of the cause of the Great Depression.

In the event, the cause of the energy gap was a decision by the US Treasury Department – and allegedly without the knowledge of the Federal Reserve – to sterilise inflows of gold into the US. Throughout 1937, an otherwise natural expansion in the money aggregates was therefore stopped. Consequently, at a time when the economy was already struggling against the headwinds of politically-motivated tax increases[97] and the phenomenon of the Dust Bowl, money growth actually contracted sharply. The monetary shock unbalanced an already vulnerable system. It is currently impossible to say why such an event happened almost exactly when it was supposed to happen. Nevertheless, the 1937–38 energy gap was an intrinsic part of the life cycle profile.

## The trigger for the 1908–1942 era

The Life Cycle Hypothesis indicates that the 1937–38 crisis triggered a new life cycle into being. Since such a second energy gap crisis occurs only every 36 years, it means that the next crisis in the sequence should have impacted in 1973–74. This is exactly what happened. By the same analysis, the 1908–42 life cycle was itself triggered by an event 36 years before the 1937–38 recession. This indicates that a creative shock should have appeared in 1901–02. In fact, there is always a small amount of leeway involved, so the practical timing is 1900–1904. According to the NBER, there was a recession between September 1902 and August 1904. There was also a 38% fall in the DJIA in 1903, which became known at the time as the 'rich man's panic'.[98] These two facts suggest that the period 1902–04 was, indeed, the source of the 1908–42 life cycle.

## The emergence of the 1908–42 life cycle

Figure 10-3 shows the resulting overlap between the Termination Cycle that contained the 1902–04 energy gap and the learning phase of the life cycle that generated the Great Depression. The heavy black line shows the momentum of the Business Activity Index; the black dashed line shows the Termination Cycle of the old life cycle; and the grey dashed line shows the learning phase of the newly-evolving life cycle. The life cycles are presented in their archetypal format (rather than terms of momentum), and so will not coincide exactly with actual events. It is nevertheless very clear that the final energy gap of the old life cycle

---

[97]   The influence of political opinion is very clear in Franklin Roosevelt's 'Message to Congress' in 1935. See: www.presidency.ucsb.edu/ws/?pid=15088. The tax increases happened at a time of low inflation and economic stagnation, and were not helpful. See, for example: object.cato.org/sites/cato.org/files/pubs/pdf/tbb-0303-14.pdf.

[98]   There was another crisis in 1907, which also came to be known as the 'rich man's panic'. It is rather like the term 'Great Depression'. The name was originally given to the depression of the 1890s, but was subsequently used to apply to the depression of the 1930s.

materialised in the form of the 1902–04 recession[99] and that the new life cycle came into being as a result.

As always, the emergence of the new life cycle consisted of three stages: (i) the reaction to a shock; (ii) an adjustment to the new set of conditions; and (iii) the emergence of a Threshold Cycle. The initiating shock was obviously the 1902/04 recession and its associated 1903 financial crisis; the learning was reflected in – and was deepened by – the 1907–08 recession and its accompanying financial crisis; and the Threshold Cycle then unfolded between 1908 and 1911.

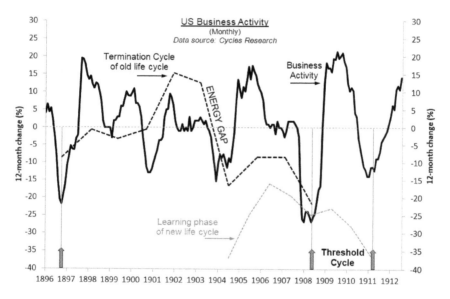

Figure 10-3: The overlap between cycles

# The 1907–08 recession

The depth of the 1907–08 recession in Figure 10-3 is very clear. As mentioned in Chapter 6, it was also accompanied by a deep correction in equities. In 1907, there was an attempt to corner shares in a copper mining company. The attempt failed, and there was a run on the associated banks. In the process, the

---

[99]   This uses the NBER's dating. However, the energy gap (and the resulting fall in the Business Activity Index) places the recession in 1903–04.

Knickerbocker Trust had to close.[100] By November 1907, the DJIA was about 50% lower than it had been in January 1906. As a result of these events, the 1907–08 experience is better known than that of 1902–04. Indeed, since the extent of the equity fall in 1906–07 was greater than that of 1903, it replaced the latter as being the 'rich man's panic'.

The irony, of course, is that the Life Cycle Hypothesis indicates the 1902–04 experience was the one that kick-started the life cycle that incorporated the Great Depression. That means that the 1902–04 recession and associated financial crisis were in some way more responsible for the Great Depression than were the events of 1907–08. The difference between the two periods is that 1902–04 delivered the information shock that triggered a new life cycle, while 1907–08 augmented the effects of that shock and ensured that the learning was permanent. The two recessions, and their associated financial traumas, underwrote the assumptions and beliefs that drove the new life cycle.

## The role of monetary policy

So what were these assumptions and beliefs? The clue to their nature was implicit in the use of the term 'rich man's panic' to reference the sharp falls in the DJIA in 1903 and 1906–07. The general opinion at the time was that both downswings mainly impacted a combination of bankers, those with money, and equity market insiders. They did not destroy the smaller investor in the same way as did the crash of 1929 and its aftermath. Nevertheless, the resulting recessions created widespread hostility towards bankers.

Quite naturally, those people who were affected by successive 'rich man's' financial panics were the ones who subsequently supported the introduction of a more centralised system. This is why, in 1910, a number of men met on Jekyll Island in order to set off the process that would eventually result in the Federal Reserve System.[101]

## The Federal Reserve System

I covered some of the conditions confronting the newly-created Federal Reserve System in Chapter 6. When the Fed was established in 1913, it was seen as being the outcome of a compromise. On the one hand, it was a decentralised central bank; on the other it was designed to balance the competing interests of private sector survival and collective antagonism towards banks. The underlying difficulty, however, was that the Federal Reserve was born in an era where the

---

100   See, for example: www.federalreservehistory.org/essays/panic_of_1907.
101   See, for example: www.federalreservehistory.org/essays/jekyll_island_conference.

prevailing approach to policy was one of minimal intervention. So, although interest rates would be raised and lowered as market circumstances dictated, the direct management of money growth was not a priority.

Figure 10-4 shows the change in the Business Activity Index (i.e., the thick line) compared with the annual percentage change in the money stock, M2 (i.e., the dashed line). The correlation between the two time series is convincing. The very serious economic contractions in 1920–21, 1929–32, and 1937–38 are clearly integrated with changes in the money supply. The only question relates to whether negative monetary growth was the **cause** of each recession, or whether negative monetary growth was an **effect** of each recession.

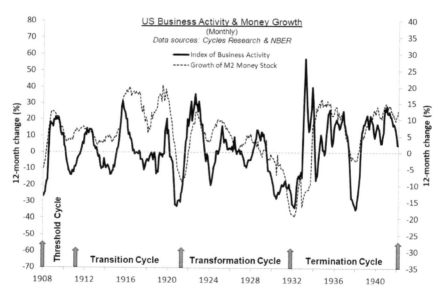

Figure 10-4: The Great Depression and money growth

# The shift in political attitudes in the 1930s

Prior to the 1929–32 collapse, the prevailing political belief was **laissez-faire**. It is therefore difficult to argue that the Fed actively **caused** the recessions.[102] Nevertheless, under Herbert Hoover and Franklin Roosevelt, the political

---

[102]    The primary failure of the Fed was their inability to differentiate between a systemic problem and moral jeopardy.

environment swung behind some form of intervention. Unfortunately, economic theory at the time was not particularly helpful: it did not fully appreciate the relationship between money growth and nominal economic activity; it did not properly recognise the influence on the economic and financial aggregates of collective behaviour; and it could not provide a notional justification for higher government spending. Lord Keynes did not publish his *General Theory* until 1936, and it would obviously have taken time for an associated paradigm shift to occur in academic understandings.[103]

Even so, it would have become increasingly obvious that something was wrong. Inevitably, therefore, politicians felt that the government ought to do something. In 1931, work on the Hoover Dam was begun; from 1932 onwards, personal and corporate taxation was progressively increased; and, in 1933, the Federal Open Market Committee (FOMC) was established. By the time that the US entered WWII, **laissez-faire** had effectively given way to the supposed advantages of government intervention.[104]

## The modern age

The modern age can be said to incorporate three eras: the Roaring Twenties and Great Depression (1908–42); the consumer revolution and the great inflation (1942–78); and the infotech revolution and the severe deflation (1978–2012/13). When these eras are presented separately, and in their original format, they reveal the presence of an evolutionary process whose main inflexion points are not random. In fact, the major shifts in direction are entirely predictable. The presence of an integral process means that the three eras can be averaged together to reveal the essential pattern of the age. All that is necessary is that we use a data series that can be applied to all three eras, and that the shorter periods are mathematically stretched to equal the duration of the longest period.

This averaging process was used to create a template for the post-war cycles of 1942–78 and 1978–2013. It was the basis of Figure 10-1. We can now add the 1908–42 era to the procedure, and the results of doing so are shown in Figure 10-5.

Obviously, the overall pattern is dominated by oscillations in business activity during the 1908–42 era. However, it is the **extent** of those oscillations that

---

[103] John Maynard Keynes, *The General Theory of Employment, Interest, and Money* (Macmillan & Co, London, 1936).

[104] It is therefore no small matter that the explosion of the nuclear bomb over Hiroshima in 1945 occurred late in the Threshold Cycle of a new socio-economic era. It confirmed the reality of US government power, and underwrote the shift to centralised authority in economics and politics.

exert an influence, not their timing. Apart from one anomaly, the timings remain in line with those that are intrinsic to the life cycle. The average shape of the Threshold Cycle, the energy gaps in the average Transition and Termination Cycles, and the average of the final downswings in the Transition, Transformation, and Termination Cycles, are exactly as predicted by the Life Cycle Hypothesis.

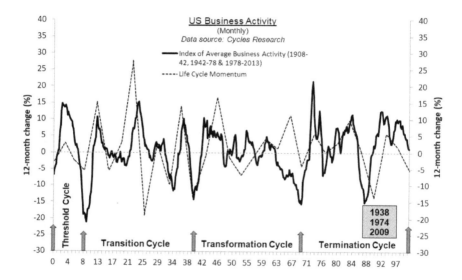

Figure 10-5: The average life cycle in the modern era

The anomaly is the fact that the average pattern does not recover when it should, at the end of the average Transformation Cycle. In the post-war life cycles, a recovery was evident; pre-war, however, it was not. The fact that economic activity failed to recover significantly between late 1929 and early 1931 was **prima facie** evidence of a major dislocation to the prevalent economic, political, and social milieu.

## Conclusion

This chapter has built on the findings of Chapter 9, which highlighted the presence of an evolutionary process in collective economic behaviour. It has been shown that this behaviour has a very specific pattern, and that this pattern can be used to predict major economic and financial turning points. It has also been shown, however, that the pattern is so fundamental to collective behaviour that major divergences are evidence of a significant dislocation. Once such a dislocation is recognised, it should be possible to identify the causes and then deal with them.

It is very obvious that normal evolutionary forces were disrupted between late 1929 and mid-1932. It appears, however, that the disturbance was caused, not by insufficient government intervention, but by a particular interpretation of **laissez-faire**. This interpretation treated the growth in the credit and money aggregates as being a result of economic activity. The growth in those aggregates might therefore have been seen as a symptom of the health (or otherwise) of the economy, but not as a target for direct intervention.

This does not, however, automatically imply that the credit and money aggregates should be treated as a **cause** of economic activity. This is the error that has dominated academic thought since Lord Keynes wrote his *General Theory*. The Life Cycle Hypothesis reveals that economic stability depends on the absence of excesses in the system. This applies to credit and money as much as to economic activity itself. Downswings in energy are as essential to growth and evolution as are upswings in energy. Problems arise when the extent of the fluctuations are driven by excesses.

In the case of the Great Depression, economic activity contracted because the credit and money aggregates imploded. Economic activity did not, however, contract because of the absence of government. Indeed, the Life Cycle Hypothesis reveals that the expansion of government is, in itself, a potential cause of instability. Such expansion doesn't just accommodate excesses, it actively embeds them in the system. One result was the inflation of the 1970s; another was the deflation of the 2000s. In a sense, therefore, the problem of the Great Depression has led to official excesses in later periods. There seems little doubt that academic economics will need to confront another major paradigm shift.

# *11*

# 10-Year US Treasury Notes

## Introduction

IT HAS ALREADY been shown that, with a sufficiently long time series, the Life Cycle Hypothesis can usefully be applied to collective behaviour in financial markets. This is a profoundly important way of identifying those turning points that are going to be significant. In Chapters 6 and 7, the focus was specifically on the Dow Jones Industrial Average in the US. In this chapter, the focus is on 10-year US Treasury Notes. This allows the introduction of a number of new concepts, which relate both to the evolutionary forces that are at work, and to the potential variability of the cycles that transmit those forces.

The important insight is that the process of evolution necessarily involves mutation. This does not just mean linear quantitative changes; it also means non-linear qualitative changes. Moreover, these qualitative changes are likely to be occurring at a deep structural level, and are therefore likely to be hidden from general view.

## A look at the data

The basic data consist of the monthly highs, lows, and closes of 10-year Treasury Note yields. Visually, it is sometimes best to see a market in price terms. Consequently, the yields have been converted to a price index by the simple expedient of deducting the yield from 100. The initial results are shown in Figure 11-1.

The graph tracks the behaviour of the index since January 1980. It therefore covers a period that has been dominated by a structural deflation, brought about by the revolution in information technology and by increased access to cheap labour in the wake of globalisation.

The peak of each advance, and the trough of each decline, have been marked with the relevant date and associated yield. This confirms the ongoing uptrend, defined as higher highs and higher lows. Moreover, the uptrend after October 1987 is contained within a pair of gradually narrowing trendlines.[105]

Figure 11-1: 10-year US Treasury Notes, 1980–present

## Detrending the data

In order to be able to see the life cycle in Treasury Notes (hereafter T-Notes), it is necessary to remove the trend from the data. There are a number of ways of doing this, but the one that I have chosen is a straightforward regression line. It is then possible to calculate a straightforward deviation from the trend. Figure 11-2 accordingly shows the straight line regression of price against time, dating from 1976. Within reason, any regression line would be practical. It is necessary only to establish a base trend for the period after 1987. The equation for this particular regression line is:

$$Y = 0.0194X + 88.941$$

---

[105] The low in Treasury-bond prices (high in yields) in October 1987, occurred just before the 1987 equity crash.

Figure 11-2: 10-year US T-Note regression, 1976–present

## The life cycle

Once this has been done, the life cycle can be brought into focus by deducting the calculated trend of the T-Note index from the actual level of that index. This is done in Figure 11-3, where the calculated locus of the T-Note is the heavy black line, the pattern of the life cycle is the dashed black line, and the momentum of the life cycle is shown as the dashed grey line. In addition, I have included vertical grey lines to coincide with the major price lows at the end of each of the underlying evolution-orientated cycles.

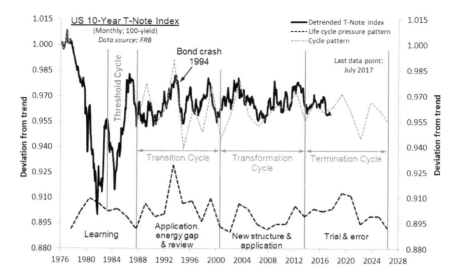

Figure 11-3: US T-Note life cycle

The preliminary learning pattern fits neatly with the violent fluctuations in the market between June 1977 and October 1987. The surge in T-Note prices up into late 1993 can be classified as a bubble. The subsequent crash in 1994 is very clear. There is then a significant three-wave recovery into late 1998, followed by a contraction into early 2000. The fact that the T-Note pattern contains a bubble-and-crash is extremely important. It confirms that the fluctuations between October 1987 and January 2000 belong to a Transition Cycle. This identifies the presence of a genuine life cycle.

## The life cycle as a pressure pattern

At this point, it is worth noting that there are divergences between actual market behaviour and the theoretical life cycle. For example, market prices stopped falling in early 2000, but the Transition Cycle pattern of the life cycle continued lower. Then, at the end of the Transformation Cycle, T-Note prices continued to fall until the end of 2013, even though the life cycle itself turned up in the late summer of 2013. These divergences are very small. Nevertheless, they imply that a life cycle should be treated as a **pressure pattern**, rather than as a mechanical oscillator. The index being tracked will almost certainly have to respond to contemporary influences as well as to the underlying life cycle.

## Duration of sub-cycles

A related implication is that a contraction in one of the three evolution-orientated cycles – i.e., in the Transition, Transformation, or Termination Cycles – will probably engender a compensating adjustment in one of the other two cycles. In this case, a contraction in the Transition Cycle has been matched by an expansion in the Transformation Cycle. This makes sense. The volatility of the Transition Cycle will encourage a rapid unwinding of excesses, while the trend element of the Transformation Cycle will encourage that cycle to last longer. Nevertheless, it is still essential to use the average of the two cycles in order to project forward into the Transition Cycle. This should ensure that the total length of the projected cycle is approximately equal to the sum of three sub-cycles of equal duration.

In the case of T-Note prices, the Transition Cycle lasted 12¼ years and the Transformation Cycle lasted for 14 years. The average cycle beat, therefore, was just over 13 years. This suggests that the Transition Cycle will end in late 2026, and that the sum of all three sub-cycles will be 39 years.

## The learning cycle

Despite the need for adjustments to the duration of each sub-cycle, there is an extremely close match between the actual behaviour of the T-Note price index and the pattern both of the archetypal life cycle and of related momentum. The obvious exception is that, during the learning phase, the T-Note index moved in the opposite direction to the life cycle. This is important. The reaction phase of this life cycle learning pattern (i.e., the rise) is associated with a collapse in the T-Note index, and the absorption phase of that learning pattern (i.e., the fall) is matched by a rise in the index. Moreover, the temporary rise in the life cycle in the middle of that absorption phase is accompanied by a sharp fall in the T-Note index.

These negative relationships emphasise the fact the learning phase is a response to developments in the external holding field. In this case, the holding field involved the control (or otherwise) of inflation. The appointment of Paul Volcker as chairman of the Federal Reserve Board was helpful, but interest rates still needed to be raised sufficiently to reassert proper control. Over short periods of time, higher official interest rates would have had a negative impact effect on the T-Note index. Over longer periods, however, the effects would have been beneficial.

Overall, the Threshold Cycle is probably as indicated in Figure 11-3. It is likely that the end of the Threshold Cycle was signalled by the rise in official interest rates, and therefore the slump in T-Note prices, ahead of the 1987 equity crash. The behaviour by the Fed indicated its commitment to lower inflation.

## The evolution of expectations

If the learning pattern is put to one side, and the theoretical duration of the Transition and Transformation Cycles are adjusted to match actual market behaviour, then the situation is as shown in Figure 11-4. Again – and to emphasise the point – the presence of a Transition Cycle is very clear. The disinflationary impact of the 1990–91 recession inspired a T-Note bubble, and this was followed by the 1994 bond crash. The subsequent three-wave advance created sufficient excesses to warrant the end-of-cycle fall in T-Note prices between late 1998 and early 2000. The main driving force behind a Transition Cycle is the need to create a genuine break with the past. This is why it is so volatile – particularly with respect to the bubble-and-crash. In this case, the T-Note market broke away from the psychology of inflation.

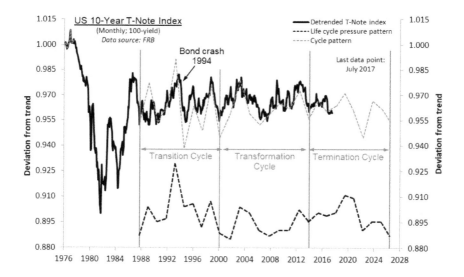

Figure 11-4: US T-Note life cycle and momentum cycles

# The Transformation Cycle

After the Transition Cycle comes the Transformation Cycle. This is when collective behaviour shifts into a new phase of learning. Attention turns away from the noticeable outer influences towards inner considerations; and, sometimes, these inner matters are not obvious. In this case, the advance in the T-Note index between January 2000 and May 2003 paralleled a major bear phase in equities. In principle, a fall in equities will reflect concern about economic activity and, as will be outlined in Chapter 14, there is evidence that the main thrust of the revolution in information technology ended around this time. Moreover, a weaker economy means that the Federal Reserve would be more likely to reflate by lowering interest rates if the evidence permitted. Not surprisingly, therefore, the T-Note index rallied as interest rates fell.

Also not surprising – at least at the time – was that interest rates rose again as the economy appeared to recover. At first the rise in yields was slow, but it gathered pace in 2004 and then continued into 2005 and 2006. Consequently, the T-Note index fell. So far, so obvious; but where was the hidden learning? In fact, it came as a response to Japanese monetary policy.

# The integration of global monetary policies

Between March 2001 and March 2006, the Bank of Japan (BoJ) supplemented its policy of zero interest rates with quantitative easing. Consequently, speculators borrowed at low Japanese interest rates, sold yen into dollars, and bought US bonds (and other assets) that had higher yields. Between January 2005 and June 2007, when this 'carry trade' had its greatest momentum, the dollar-yen rose by 22%. Each rise in US interest rates therefore created a greater effective stimulus. The BoJ exited from its QE programme in 2006, but by then the damage had been done: the Fed's monetary policy had been undermined by the BoJ's monetary policy and markets were left overstretched. The 2007–09 financial crisis was the worst in living memory.

The fact that Western monetary policies had become closely integrated was subsequently emphasised by the adoption of QE by the Fed, by the European Central Bank, by the Bank of England, and (again) by the Bank of Japan. In part, the official purchase of bonds held by the private sector was helpful for the beleaguered banking system. On the other hand, however, QE raised the spectre of a return of inflation. Between December 2008 and March 2011, therefore, the T-Note index made little upside progress. However, as Western economies slipped back into the terminal junctures of their life cycles (see, for example, Chapter 9), the T-Note index rallied sharply.

Such rallies create excesses, and the co-ordinated attempt by central banks to collapse bond yields only made matters worse. So, when there were signs of a recovery in business activity in 2013, the T-Note index fell sharply. As Figure 11-4 shows, this drop brought the Transformation Cycle to an end. Since the cycle started in January 2000 and ended in December 2013, it had lasted almost 14 years.

## From transformation into termination

This means that the 10-year US T-Note market is now – at the time of writing, in summer 2017 – in the Termination Cycle of a life cycle that started in October 1987 and will end sometime in 2026. This is shown in Figure 11-5, which depicts the last stages of the Transformation Cycle and the situation to date with the currently unfolding Termination Cycle. At this stage, it is not necessary to show the life cycle pattern itself, so the chart shows only the detrended T-Note index in the form of the heavy black line and the momentum of the life cycle as the dashed grey line.

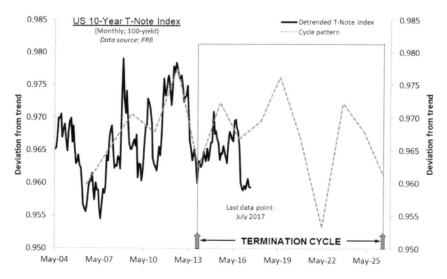

Figure 11-5: The Termination Cycle

This particular chart reveals the close correlation between the **trend** in market activity and life cycle momentum. It cannot track the detailed fluctuations but, within the overall upswing of the Transformation Cycle, it does capture the fall between December 2008 and March 2011. Moreover, it captures the high of July 2012 and the subsequent vicious setback.

Once they start, Termination Cycles are driven, not by new ideas, but by old ideas that are taken as being true. Aggressive activity based on these old ideas will inevitably create excesses, and these excesses can only be unwound by an end-of-process energy gap. In this sense, Termination Cycles are **trial and error** cycles: the strong advance is the 'trial', while the energy gap and its aftermath reflects the 'error'. Importantly, therefore, Figure 11-5 suggests that the trial phase is not yet over and that the error phase still lies ahead.

## Contemporaneous influences

We can look at the Termination Cycle in 10-year US T-Note prices in a little more detail because it throws up a number of practical considerations. It is apparent from Figure 11-5 that actual market behaviour has a degree of independence from the archetypal pattern. The fall in T-Note prices between July 2016 and January 2017 was significant. It is therefore worth repeating that the life cycle pattern relates to energy pressures rather than to actual outcomes. This means two things. Firstly, a reversal in energy allows the market itself to reverse. Secondly, a moderation in the energetic trend allows the market to react to contemporaneous events. Both influences are apparent in Figure 11-5. The downswing in the energy pattern between summer 2015 and autumn 2016 was always going to have a depressing effect on T-Note prices. Furthermore, the weak recovery in the energy pattern after autumn 2016 allowed T-Note prices to continue their fall.

This latter effect is shown in more detail in Figure 11-6, where the energy pattern between autumn 2016 and spring 2022 is divided into four more or less equal sections. The upturn in the energy pattern immediately after the 2015–16 fall is relatively modest. It therefore classifies as being 'weak' and not necessarily dominant. This helps to explain why T-Note prices have fallen so much. The upswing does, however, become 'strong' after spring 2018. So, whatever happens in the second half of 2017 and the early part of 2018, the energy trend will almost certainly force T-Note prices higher. The nature of the Termination Cycle suggests that the advance will be very speculative. This will establish the conditions for a pronounced reversal.

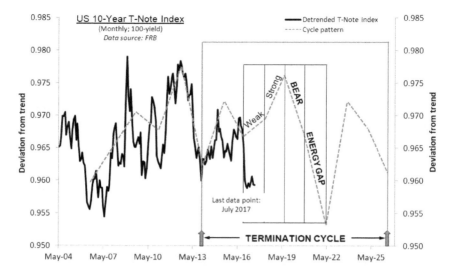

Figure 11-6: Forthcoming behaviour in T-Note prices

## The recovery and the energy gap

Figures 11-5 and 11-6 strongly suggest that the drive towards reflation is still incomplete. Specifically, the charts indicate that the peak of the Termination Cycle is not due until spring/summer 2019. Of course, the peak could arrive sooner or later than that, but the unavoidable implication is that a period of slower economic growth and of coordinated reflation still lay ahead. Certainly, the behaviour of the T-Note index since December 2013 is more consistent with the start of the Termination Cycle than with its peak.

These conclusions reflect those of Chapter 9. There it was argued that business activity was scheduled to reach a peak in the first half of 2017,[106] followed by weakness into 2018–19. Figures 11-5 and 11-6 show that an advance in T-Note prices could end around that time. On the face of it, therefore, a weak economy will encourage official reflation and rising T-Note prices. However, sometime after the economy bottoms out, a major downswing in T-Note prices will begin. Since any genuine recovery in business activity may be the prelude to a return of endemic inflation, that downswing is likely to have secular implications.

---

[106] As of summer 2017.

# Conclusion

This chapter has applied the life cycle momentum pattern to the performance of 10-year US T-Note prices since their low of October 1987. The correlation between the life cycle pattern and detrended price behaviour is compelling. It provides strong evidence for the existence of a blueprint that organises collective behaviour, and it suggests that in the T-Note market this behaviour oscillates with a 13-year rhythm. This means that contemporary assumptions about rational behaviour by economic agents, and about the necessary involvement of governments, are wrong. Individuals are neither wholly rational nor wholly separate. Moreover government activity is a part of collective behaviour.

The inference is that economic theory will need to undergo a paradigm shift in the coming years. The predicted performance of T-Note prices could provide a motivation for that shift. Economic activity will again slow, governments will respond yet again, and T-Note prices will rise. The message, however, will increasingly become that official attempts to stimulate business activity do not work. Indeed, in this particular cycle, such stimulation will generate inflation and spawn a collapse in T-Note prices.

# 12

## The 54-Year Kondratyev
## Price Cycle

### Introduction

T HE OBSERVABLE PRESENCE of regular fluctuations and recurring patterns – both in financial markets and in the economy – imply an improvement in our ability to predict the future. Nevertheless, the phenomena are not regarded with much affection by economic theorists. Not only are patterned cycles difficult to justify on the grounds of rational behaviour by independent individuals, but their presence refutes the political imperative to offset errors in that behaviour.

In recent years, even those who believe that cycles exist have been seduced by economic theory into believing that oscillations in prices and in business activity are correlated phenomena. The result has been the belief in a long-term economic cycle that has a variable periodicity of 40- to 60-years. This may, of course, be true; but it is not very helpful. The idea of such a variable **wave** is extremely difficult to apply either to our understandings of contemporaneous conditions or to the future evolution in those conditions.

In recent years, many observers have challenged the basic presumptions of economic theory, and have queried the validity of conflating prices and output. There have, for example, been long periods of time when the momentum of prices has moved in the opposite direction to the momentum of business activity. Innovations, for example, have introduced deflation and simultaneously boosted output. Moreover, persistent government intervention has inflated prices and depressed output.

Even beyond these difficulties, however, there is a basic criticism that can no longer be avoided. This is that changes in prices have a **different periodicity** to changes in output. Consequently, any attempt to treat prices and output as different sides of the same coin produces outcomes that look random, but are not. In fact, any apparent randomness tends to disappear when prices are treated independently of output. In Chapter 9, we identified the presence of a 36-year cycle in business activity. This chapter reveals the existence of a 54-year cycle in US wholesale prices.

## A preliminary look at the data

Each month, the U.S. Bureau of Labor Statistics produces an index covering all wholesale prices. It is known as the All-Commodities Producer Price Index, and the full data set goes back to January 1913.[107] Unfortunately, this leaves a significant gap relating to earlier data. Fortunately, there are longer time series available from other sources, and these can be concatenated on to the official data. The US All-Commodities Price Index used in this analysis goes back to 1743.

In order to be able to see the oscillations in this index, it is to some extent necessary to remove the underlying trend. There are many ways of doing this, but here we shall just use a two-year percentage change. This has the advantage of reducing the apparent random element in the price movements.

In the analysis that follows, I shall use the terms 'commodity prices' and 'wholesale prices' interchangeably.

## The 54-year Kondratyev Price Cycle

The 54-year cycle in commodity prices can be called the Kondratyev Price Cycle, after the Russian economist Nikolai Kondratyev. He was killed sometime during Stalin's Great Purge of 1936–38 for suggesting that the so-called capitalist system may contain self-correcting mechanisms. In fact, Kondratyev was correct: there does seem to be a long-term cycle in price fluctuations. More precisely, there is a price cycle that lasts for 54 years.[108]

Figure 12-1 shows that the first important trough in the available data is 1785, and the last important peak is 1974. A simple calculation shows that the passage of time between the two dates allows for three and a half beats of a 54-year cycle. By extension, four complete beats, starting from 1785, would end in 2001. As we shall see, there was actually a low in 2002.

---

107   U.S. Bureau of Labor Statistics, Producer Price Index for All Commodities [PPIACO], retrieved from Federal Reserve Bank of St. Louis: https://fred.stlouisfed.org/series/PPIACO, April 21, 2017.
108   The number 54 can be found in the diagram in Appendix I.

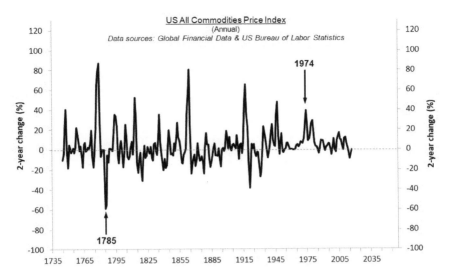

Figure 12-1: US wholesale price inflation, 1743–present

## Highs and lows in the data

Figure 12-2 shows the oscillations in the official wholesale price index, defined in terms of a 54-year periodicity. Each beat of the cycle will be subject to its own contemporaneous influences; nevertheless, there is a definite consistency in the cycle. Successive lows occurred in 1785, 1840, 1894, 1949, and 2002. These are durations, respectively, of 55 years, 54 years, 55 years, and 53 years. The average cycle length measured from low to low is therefore 54 years, and the difference from this average is only ± 1 year. This reliability – which is relatively unusual for cycles in collective behaviour – suggests that the next major low is due in 2055–57.

This evidence is enhanced by the fact that successive highs are, on average, also 54 years apart. They occur in 1758, 1813, 1864, 1917, and 1974. These represent durations of 55 years, 51 years, 53 years, and 57 years. Allowing for the historical variability of the cycle, the next momentum high in US wholesale prices is due in 2025–28.

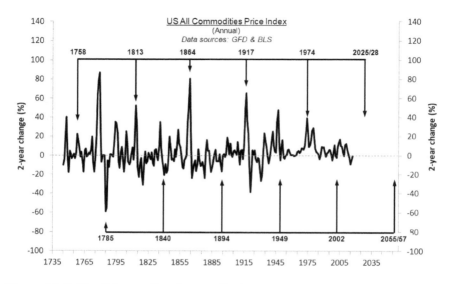

Figure 12-2: The 54-year Kondratyev Cycle

## The role of warfare

It is relevant that highs in the 54-year Kondratyev Price Cycle have invariably occurred during periods of conflict: the 1758 high involved the French and Indian War in North America; that of 1813 occurred during the Napoleonic Wars in Europe, but was specifically connected to the Anglo-American War; the high of 1864 implicates the American Civil War; the peak in 1917 was related to WWI; and the peak of 1974 occurred during the Vietnam War.

It makes sense that commodity prices and warfare are closely related. Government spending increases while supply becomes constrained, and there is a tendency to finance war budgets through printing money. Unfortunately, however, it is more difficult to make a case for a 54-year rhythm in major conflicts. And, of course, conflicts do not just come around every 54 years. WWII, for example, was a separate phenomenon. Nevertheless, the fact remains that there is a 54-year periodicity in the data.

## The average 54-year cycle

We can now look at the average pattern since 1785 of the 54-year Kondratyev Price Cycle, and then compare it with the pattern of the archetypal life cycle. Firstly, though, we need to make some simple adjustments to the data. The cycles of 1840–94 and 1949–2002 are a little shorter than those of 1785–1840 and 1894–1949. They need, therefore, to be stretched mathematically to make them equal to the other two.[109] All cycles can then be averaged together. The resulting average is shown in Figure 12-3.

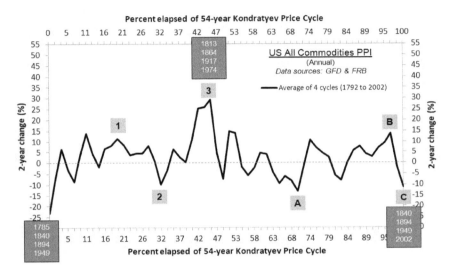

Figure 12-3: The average Kondratyev Price Cycle

In the diagram, the average cycle is centred (more or less) around the mid-cycle highs of 1813, 1864, 1917, and 1974. To the left of the high, there is a three-wave advance; while, to the right, there is a (somewhat laboured) three-wave decline. I have denoted these moves 1-2-3 and A-B-C, although opinions may vary as to the exact points at which each wave ends. The elapse of time in a cycle can then be tracked along either of the horizontal axes.

## Forecasting with the 54-year price cycle

The constancy of the US wholesale price cycle, both in its shape and in its duration, is extraordinary. It means that it can be used for forecasting. All that needs to be done is that the unfolding of any new cycle is tracked against the average. Figure 12-4 accordingly shows the pattern of behaviour in commodity

---

109 I have used the same method to stretch the shorter cycles as was used to equalise the duration of output cycles in Chapter 10.

price momentum since the 2002 low, set against the average cycle (i.e., measured across four cycles).

The time axis for the post-2002 cycle (black line with grey diamonds) is now shown along the top horizontal axis. The chart shows that there was a rise and fall in commodity prices between 2002 and 2009. These two dates marked the lows of two successive financial crises. The chart also shows the behaviour of commodity prices after 2009. There was a recovery followed by a pronounced deflationary fall into 2015. At the time of writing (summer 2017), a recovery in inflation seems to be underway, which should persist during 2017. But the important message is that this recovery is actually a prelude to another bout of weakness in wholesale prices.

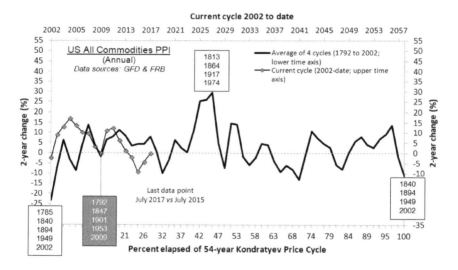

Figure 12-4: The pattern since 2002

The obvious questions are: when might the next low materialise, and what in any case might be going on at this stage of the cycle? The first point to be taken from Figure 12-4 is that the lows of 2002 and 2009 were not entirely unique. Such lows seem to materialise in pairs. There were lows in 1785 and 1792, 1840 and 1847, 1894 and 1901, and 1949 and 1953. Of these the 1949 and 1953 lows were only four years apart, but all the others – including the time lag between the lows of 2002 and 2009 – were seven years apart. So, if we assume that the recovery from WWII was sufficiently difficult to distort behaviour, it is probably also correct to assume that the natural lag between the start of the 54-year cycle and its first interim low is actually seven years.

## Introducing the time lag

This is important, because it means that the life cycle pattern can be overlaid on the 54-year cycle, but without including the first seven years of the latter. In other words, the two successive lows produce a systemic reaction that then leads into a major paradigm shift. I suspect that the double low phenomenon – and, in particular, the second low when compared with the first – becomes, in effect, a creative shock.

In Figure 12-5, therefore, the archetypal life cycle pattern (dashed black line) is overlaid on the average pattern of the fluctuations in commodity prices, but starting from the second of the two lows – i.e., from 1792, 1847, 1901, 1953, and 2009. The correlations are extraordinary, but reflect the findings of earlier chapters. They mean that the life cycle of change, which is generated by the phenomenon of the double low, lasts for 47 years.

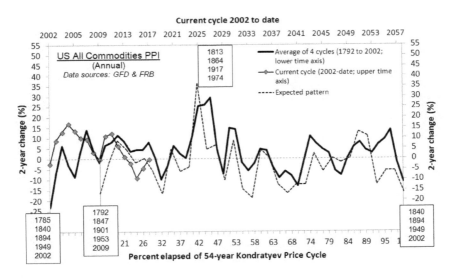

Figure 12-5: The life cycle pattern

## Systemic differences

The creative shock that generates a full life cycle pattern is thus different for commodity prices than it is for industrial output. In the case of prices, the creative shock is a double low that occurs well after the previous inflation cycle has finished; in the case of industrial output (which was discussed in Chapter 9), the creative shock is the end-of-cycle energy gap. In a sense, therefore, an inflation shock to prices is exogenous to the system being tracked, whereas the output shock can be seen as being endogenous.

This difference is fundamental. It highlights the importance of treating prices and output as separate phenomena, but we can also note here that it also says something important about the nature of government. The use of a life cycle pattern to track collective behaviour reveals that one of the most important influences on inflation is government policy. Bursts of monetary inflation have, in the past, involved some combination of warfare and significant increases in the supply of money and credit. However, in the past, such events have not been driven by the rhythms of economic life; they have, instead, been a reaction to external events.

In a sense, therefore, inflation shocks have not been 'systemic'. This contrasts with economic activity, whose fluctuations do seem to be part of a systemic process. Economic oscillations may be magnified by government policy and/ or by external events, but the **timing** of turning points in those oscillations remains more or less constant.

These differences between the inflation cycle of 54 years and the output cycle of 36 years are observable. Nevertheless, they do not resolve one important issue, which is the question of the pacemakers that are at work. At this point, all that can be offered is that we do not yet know the nature of all the forces to which we are subject.

## The learning process

Despite this gap in our knowledge, we can still track the momentum of wholesale prices within the context of its proposed life cycle. Hence, as of summer 2017, it appears that the commodity markets are still undergoing a learning process. This process started at the 2009 low, just as it did in 1792, 1847, 1901, and 1953. Initially, there is a simple upwards reaction that does not alter the underlying belief structure. Then there is the adjustment process that alters long-term beliefs in order to reduce system stress. The last phase of this whole process is a Threshold Cycle. This cycle generates sufficient disappointment and uncertainty to ensure that collective psychology is prepared to accept some form of change. Its location is shown in Figure 12-6.

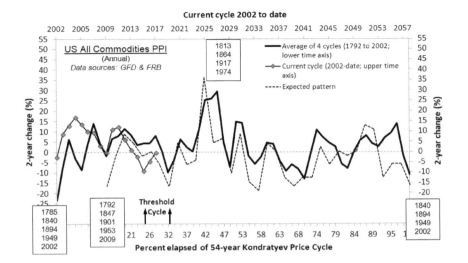

Figure 12-6: Threshold to inflation

The onset of evolution is therefore registered – either just before or just after the end of the Threshold Cycle – by an overt signal confirming that the system is ready for change. Obviously, the recognition of such a signal is a matter of interpretation. Indeed, it can often be recognised only after the event. Even so, given the relationship between inflation and conflict, it is possible to see the relevance of events such as: (i) the establishment in 1802 of the West Point Military Academy ahead of the war a decade later; (ii) the legal judgement in 1857 that African-Americans were not citizens of the US, plus the attack in 1859 by the slave abolitionist John Brown, in the run-up to the American Civil War; (iii) the meeting on Jekyll Island in 1910 that led to the creation of the Federal Reserve System, and the election in 1912 of Woodrow Wilson who was president when the US entered WWI; and (iv) the election in 1960 of John F. Kennedy, and his deployment in 1961 of US troops to Vietnam.

## Inflation and conflict

The forthcoming low of the Threshold Cycle should reprise the lows of 1802, 1858, 1911, and 1962. As Figure 12-7 shows, this next low is due in 2019. Its significance is that, once it has been registered, it will signal a shift into a more inflationary environment. Moreover, the low has usually also anticipated more military action: the peak momentum in commodity prices during the Anglo-American War (1812–15) was registered in 1813; there was a peak during the

American Civil War (1861–65) in 1864; the highs of WWI (1914–18) were reached in 1917; and the last peak in commodity price inflation was reached during the US's involvement in the Vietnam War (1965–75) in 1974.

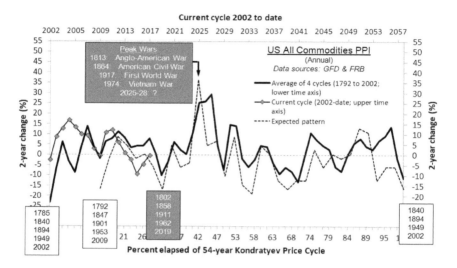

Figure 12-7: Inflation and conflict

# A commodity price bubble

A Threshold Cycle usually already contains the seeds of a forthcoming bubble: widening investor participation, accelerating momentum, and some form of justification as to why it should continue. Inevitably, the advance has been rapid over a relatively short period of time. Historically, commodity price bubbles have been driven by rising government spending and a bias towards monetary financing of the resulting budget deficit. The unavoidable conclusion is that governments create inflationary bubbles.

It will therefore be important to watch for a signal that registers a shift in collective consciousness towards accepting rising inflation and an intensification of international hostilities. In all probability, such a signal has not yet been generated, although the preconditions are certainly in place. There is now a strong political desire to stimulate inflation via monetary growth, and there has been a general increase in global aggression and militancy. So, the need to watch political conditions is now very strong. At the moment, the Life Cycle

Hypothesis indicates that the next peak in commodity prices is likely to occur in the time frame of 2025–2028.

## Subsequent disinflation

A bubble is inevitably followed by a crash of some sort. This is the **first** energy gap in the life cycle process. No matter how justified were the causes of the preceding bubble, the system attempts to unwind the resulting excesses and starts the process of diverting attention to other objectives. Figure 12-8 indicates that, historically, this readjustment phase has lasted for about two years. Only on one occasion (1917–21) was it longer: in 1920, the **laissez-faire** administration of Woodrow Wilson cut the size of the public sector and, in 1921, Wilson's policy was continued by the administration led by Warren Harding. In the current political environment, which depends on high levels of government spending, a short time period seems likely.

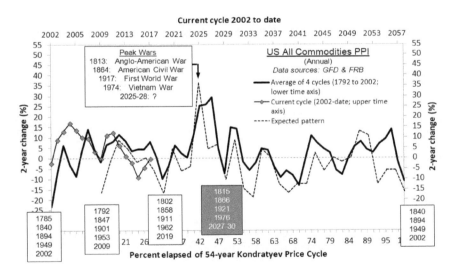

Figure 12-8: Disinflation

Obviously, though, any forecast concerning the post-bubble low will depend: (a) on the timing of the high itself; and (b) on how the US government reacts to the conditions that will emerge in the next few years. At the moment, the scheduled high consists of a range rather than a precise date. Moreover, we cannot yet know in detail the forces of global aggression that are currently gestating. However, if the commodity price high occurs during the time window of 2025–28, and the price collapse then takes two years, a major low is likely between 2027 and 2030.

## The aftermath

Sudden sharp falls in any market are usually followed by a technical bounce based on the closing of trading positions. Commodity price markets are no exception, so the collapse phase will be followed by a recovery of some sort. This is not, however, the end of the readjustment. Many market participants will have been taken by surprise and, in the case of commodity prices, the economic forces associated with the prior inflation will largely have been removed. Consequently, the downward pressures on inflation will persist.

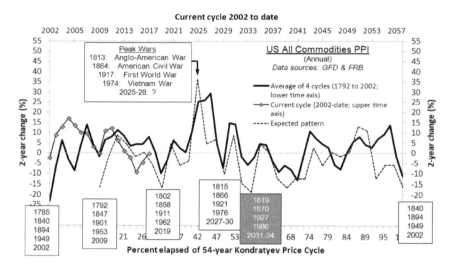

Figure 12-9: Persistent disinflation

This is one of the aspects of energy gaps – and of financial crashes – that is often missed. The crash itself does not remove all the excesses; there is a process to be navigated. In the past, therefore, commodity price inflation has subsided again. Figure 12-9 shows that, in previous cycles this happened in 1819, 1870, 1927, and 1986. The lag seems to have become longer through time, increasing from three years to ten years as the US's global power expanded. However, in all cases, there was a re-test of the sell-off lows. If this rhythm continues, commodity prices should eventually re-test their 2027–30 lows sometime in the early 2030s.

## Changed psychology

The timing of this re-test will depend partly on the timing of the preceding inflation peak, and partly on the degree to which inflation expectations have become entrenched. However, there is something very important about the re-test period that needs to be recognised. This is that the combination of the removal of conflict and an energy gap in inflation has a profound effect on collective psychology. There is a boost to confidence.

Figure 12-10 shows the sequence of post-conflict elation, placed in their historical contexts. The first example is the Era of Good Feelings of 1815–28 that emerged after the War of 1812.[110] The second is the Gilded Age of 1866–1878 that followed the American Civil War.[111] The third period is that of the Roaring Twenties of 1920–29, which came after WWI and official spending cuts.[112] And then there was the Reagan Era or Reagan Revolution of 1981–88, which eventually materialised after the Vietnam War.[113] Often, of course, the dates that are given will differ between authors, because little or no recognition is given to the impact of the 54-year cycle. However, once the underlying rhythm has been seen, it becomes too obvious to be ignored. It looks as if the next such period will emerge in the 2030s.

---

110  The phrase "Era of Good Feelings" was first used by Benjamin Russell, in the Boston Federalist newspaper, *Columbian Centinel*, in 1817. This followed President Monroe's visit to Boston, Massachusetts. See, e.g., George Dangerfield, *The Era of Good Feelings* (Harcourt, Brace & Co., New York, 1952).

111  The term "Gilded Age" came from a novel by the same name, written by Mark Twain. See, eg, *Calhoun, Charles W., ed. The Gilded Age: Perspectives on the Origins of Modern America* (Rowman & Littlefield, New York, 2007).

112  See, e.g., Frederick L Allen, *Only Yesterday: An Informal History of the Nineteen-Twenties* (Harper and Rowe, New York, 1931). A free download is available at http://xroads.virginia.edu/~HYPER/ALLEN/Cover.html.

113  See, eg, Doug Rossinow, *The Reagan Era: A History of the 1980s* (Columbia University Press, New York, 2015). Disinflationary growth was slow to materialise after the Vietnam War because of the degree to which inflation had become entrenched in the economy.

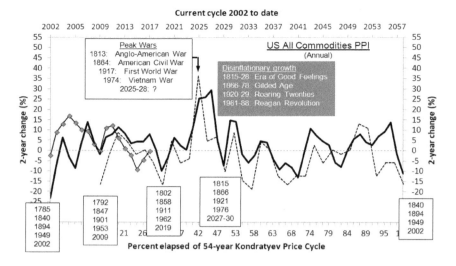

Figure 12-10: Disinflationary growth

## Conclusion

There is a 54-year cycle inherent in US wholesale prices. It is not the only cycle, but it is important. Moreover, it conforms to the periodicity indicated by Nikolai Kondratyev. The lows of this cycle are particularly regular. They vary from the average periodicity only by ± 1 year. The highs of the cycle occur with a slightly more variable periodicity, but their incidence is related to conflict and to the monetary financing of that conflict. It is an unavoidable conclusion of this analysis, therefore, that government is responsible for periodic outbreaks of uncontrollable inflation.

These outbreaks can be anticipated because the whole cycle is based upon a fundamental evolutionary process. The first seven years or so of the cycle are involved in creating an information shock that sets a much longer-term process in motion. Commodity users and suppliers learn both that a change is taking place, and that this change is potentially inflationary. Consequently, when a conflict does emerge, commodity price inflation jumps sharply higher.

This surge in inflation has similar characteristics to a 'bubble', and therefore generates an unusually pronounced high. It is invariably followed by an energy gap that has the same identifying features as a 'crash'. This energy gap normally lasts about two years. However, since it is usually associated with the withdrawal of military spending, it sets off a change in the environment that is characterised by collective optimism.

This whole cycle is so clear, and so repetitive, that it is surprising that it has not yet been observed by economic historians. One of the more obvious problems is that no one has yet successfully isolated a valid pacemaker for the observable periodicity. In the meantime, a life cycle approach can be used to anticipate future developments by tracking the current pattern against the average historical pattern.

# *13*

# The Future Of The Euro

## Introduction

ONE OF THE important insights of the Life Cycle Hypothesis is that the second half of a life cycle starts with the incorporation of new knowledge. There has been an energy gap and the system – or organism – will need to adjust to it. This usually means that the system switches its focus from external structures to internal processes. The switch is often so subtle that it is either missed or ignored. It is, however, the foundation for another move forward.

As of summer 2017, the euro valued in terms of the US dollar has probably entered just such an adjustment phase. It is obvious to most commentators that the beliefs around which the euro was originally constructed have run into strong headwinds. On the one hand, some countries within the euro-zone have had to deflate internally because they cannot deflate externally. Their inability to devalue, in other words, implies low wage growth and high unemployment. On the other hand, the European Central Bank has been trying to devalue the euro-dollar by imposing historically low interest rates and by keeping money markets as liquid as possible. In theory, the overall result should be a boost to growth. However, central banks outside the euro-zone have also been trying to apply a monetary stimulus and benefit from a depreciated currency. The result, in effect, has been an impasse.

Nevertheless, an analysis of the euro-dollar's life cycle reveals that a subtle change in opinion is probably taking place – both amongst the nations that participate in the euro-zone, and amongst the authorities that manage the structural arrangements. This change should allow either a quick reaction to a crisis or the modification of existing arrangements to forestall a crisis. But some form of practical change is now virtually unavoidable. It is just a question of when – and under what conditions – the necessary adjustments can actually be made.

## Early origins

The euro-dollar (hereafter 'euro'), officially came into being on 1 January 1999. This moment of birth was, however, the end phase of a long gestation period. Obviously the appropriate institutional arrangements had to be made, the markets had to be ready actively to trade the euro, and the so-called 'legacy' currencies of the nations participating in the euro-zone had to find a fixed relationship with the new currency.

The proposals for the euro were presented to the European Commission by the Delors Committee in June 1988, and were officially accepted in June 1989. The free movement of capital (Phase I of the transition) began in July 1990. The convergence of the legacy currencies (Phase II) then began in January 1994. And the actual launch of the Euro (Phase III) occurred in January 1999. So there was a lag of almost ten years between the acceptance of the proposals and the actual implementation of those proposals. In between, of course, there was the signing, in February 1992, of the Maastricht Treaty.

## Behaviour of the euro

This diversity of dates automatically provides a range of potential starting points for the euro. However, there is obviously a difference between conception, gestation, and birth. So, the question is: at what point did collective behaviour in the markets start to react to the bureaucratic changes that were underway?

Figure 13-1 shows the end-month value of the euro in terms of the US dollar. Prior to 1 January 1999, the value of the euro is the notional one calculated from legacy currencies by the Bank of England.[114] After 1 January 1999, the monthly values of the euro are the ones that have been determined by the market. It is quite obvious that, in its early stages, the process of getting used to the new currency was not necessarily easy. Early strength in European currencies after the acceptance of the Delors Proposals was interrupted by a bout of weakness once the free movement of capital came into effect. The eventual high in August 1992 was then followed by a prolonged three-phase decline. At its closing monthly low in May 2001, the euro was almost 45% lower than it had been in August 1992.

---

[114]   Prior to 1999, a synthetic euro exchange rate has been calculated by geometrically weighting the bilateral exchange rates of the (then) eleven euro area countries using "weights" based on the country shares of extra euro-area trade.

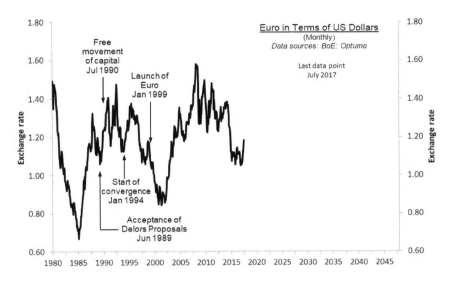

Figure 13-1: The euro basket against the dollar after 1980

## The euro's life cycle

There is some evidence that changes in market behaviour began when the free movement of capital was allowed within the proposed euro-zone. Nevertheless, the start date of that free movement – July 1990 – may not have been the actual 'birth' date of the euro's life cycle. It almost certainly took some time for investors collectively to adjust their portfolios in favour of the forthcoming euro, rather than in favour of the individual currencies that would constitute the euro. By June 1991, the basket of legacy currencies that would eventually form the euro was about 13% below the levels of July 1990. Indeed, when June 1991 is used as the effective 'birth' date of the single currency, rather than its actual launch date, then the subsequent fluctuations begin to make sense.

Figure 13-2 shows the profile of an archetypal life cycle (dashed line) overlaid on the synthetic and actual value after 1980 of the euro (heavy black line). The life cycle is assumed to start in or around June 1991. This means that it should finish in early 2043, making the duration of the life cycle about 52 years. Interestingly, this is compatible with the 54-year Kondratyev Price Cycle that was discussed in Chapter 12.

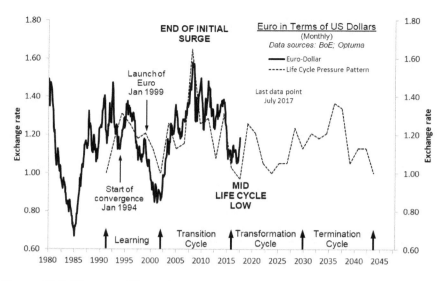

Figure 13-2: The euro life cycle

## The structure of change

The placing of the life cycle in this way – without making any adjustments to the cycle to compensate for changes in the speed of actual behaviour – indicates a number of important correlations. Firstly, the Threshold Cycle within the overall learning phase looks conventional. It consists of the rally from spring/summer 1997 to autumn 1998, and then the fall between autumn 1998 and early 2002. Secondly, the surge into the peak has a characteristic three-wave pattern: there is a rise from early 2002 to late 2004; then there is a correction; and, finally, there is a strong advance from autumn 2005 to spring 2008. On the basis of the life cycle pattern, we can classify the last stage of the surge as being a 'bubble'. Thirdly, the subsequent fall in the euro consists of three phases. The first, which runs from spring 2008 to early summer 2010 is, in effect, the 'crash' phase. Then there is the recovery phase which lasts from summer 2010 to spring 2014. Finally, there is the breakdown phase, which lasts from spring 2014 to autumn 2015.

## The Transition Cycle

Some of these observations are confirmed in Figure 13-3, where the behaviour of the euro is converted into six-month percentage changes (dark line), and then compared with the unfolding of the life cycle (dashed line). On the basis of six-month momentum, we can identify the learning phase of the life cycle pattern as starting naturally in June 1991 and ending in January 2002. Within this, the Threshold Cycle began in April 1997 and lasted until January 2002.

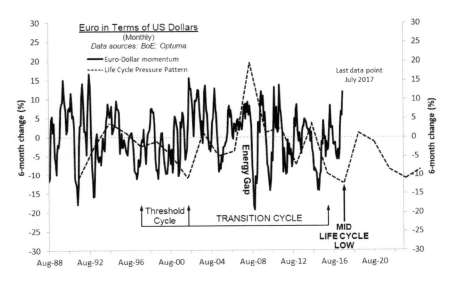

Figure 13-3: The Transition Cycle

The end of the Threshold Cycle simultaneously defines the start of the Transition Cycle. The primary function of the latter is to drag the system away from its previous structures and beliefs. In the case of the newly-formed euro, it takes very little imagination to know that this was an essential part of the process. So, if the structure of the proposed Transition Cycle matches the archetypal pattern, then we can assume that the euro has indeed been following a natural pathway.

Figure 13-3 confirms that the euro has been negotiating a pattern that looks remarkably like a bubble-and-crash. First, there was a three-phase advance between January 2002 and March 2008. The initial rise and fall, and then the final bubble stage into the March 2008 high, come across very clearly.[115] Second, this peak was followed by an **energy gap**. Such gaps underlie a crash. Since a bubble-and-crash phenomenon is an essential part of a Transition Cycle, we

[115] Given that this is a moment of some importance for the market, technical analysts will recognise that there is a non-confirmation between the April 2003 momentum high and the March 2008 momentum high.

have a justification for denoting the euro's performance between January 2002 and sometime in 2015 as being consistent with a Transition Cycle.

## Into the Transformation Cycle

It is always difficult to use just the inflexion in momentum to isolate the exact timing of a turning point. The momentum of an index will turn before the absolute level of that index. In the case of the euro, for example, the final downswing of the momentum cycle bottomed out in March 2015, but the index itself did not reach a low until November/December 2015. This is a classic example of a non-confirmation.[116] So we often need to wait, even though it is apparent from a life cycle that a change is taking place.

This is particularly true while collective behaviour is shifting from a Transition Cycle to a Transformation Cycle. As indicated in Chapter 3, the interval between the start of the Transformation Cycle and the mid-point of the whole life cycle is a period that can incorporate a spill-over from the trauma of the Transition Cycle. This seems to have happened with the euro. As Figures 13-2 revealed, the period between November 2015 and December 2016 saw the euro move sideways, with notable periods of weakness. Figure 13-3 shows that upside momentum has increased sharply since the end of 2016. This strongly suggests that the learning phase of the second half of the whole life cycle is now underway.

## The future pathway for the euro

Figure 13-4 shows this situation in a little more detail. The chart compares the level of the euro (dark line) with the unfolding of a life cycle pressure pattern (dashed line), from just before the end of the latter's Transition Cycle. Because of the overall scale of the diagram, it cannot show the relationship between the euro and its underlying life cycle with a great degree of accuracy. What it can show, however, is something very much more important – namely, the expected pressures on the direction of the euro over the next quarter of a century. This is not something that can be achieved easily with conventional economic analysis.

---

[116]  There is always the chance that the index will make a new high or low. If the momentum indicator does not follow suit, this will likely form the basis of a non-confirmed turning point.

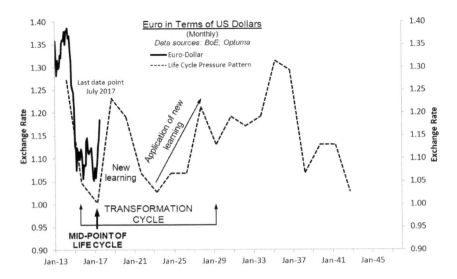

Figure 13-4: The Transformation Cycle

The first point is that the patterns confirm that the euro is: (a) in a Transformation Cycle; (b) probably beyond the halfway point of the whole life cycle; and (c) therefore almost certainly in the initial rising phase of the Transformation Cycle.

The second point follows from this. The initial rise is a prelude to what could be a much more challenging period. Much now depends on developments during the next 12 months or so. If any advance in the euro reflects changes to its constituent parts, then the advance will be genuine; if, however, the euro just rallies because the US dollar falls (for example), then the period 2018–23 could become extremely difficult. Without voluntary changes, the markets themselves will force the issue.

## The need for change

The third point, therefore, is very simple. The Transformation Cycle is all about deep-structure change and about progress. The cycle necessarily starts with an alteration in working processes and associated beliefs, and its subsequent dynamism involves the application of those adjustments. Without essential changes, there can be no proper evolution. The implication is that forward progress has its own natural pathway. Governments can alter the structure of that pathway, they can encourage periodic diversions, and they can change the speed of travel. But they cannot change the direction of the path itself. So (to pursue the metaphor a bit further) putting up road-blocks is more likely to lead to disaster than to creative development. This is the great threat that faces the euro-zone.

## Conclusion

The euro was launched, as the official currency for the euro-zone, on 1 January 1999. However, the creative shock that altered market behaviour probably occurred earlier – sometime shortly after July 1990, when the free movement of capital within the prospective euro-zone began. Given that market participants would have taken time to adjust to the new freedoms, the subsequent date for the birth of a functional life cycle is likely to have been June 1991.

Even so, there was still a learning process to be negotiated. If we place the profile of the life cycle against actual market behaviour, the end of the learning phase probably occurred in January 2002. There was then a very rapid rise in the euro. This included a notable burst of enthusiasm between November 2005 and March 2008. The rise was, however, followed by a sharp fall between March 2008 and November 2008. The fall was an energy gap, which accordingly started the process of bringing the first half of the life cycle to an end.

The combination of an extended advance followed by an energy gap is the essential characteristic of a Transition Cycle. Once that cycle has reached its end point, therefore, something quite specific happens – evolution changes its focus from external structures to internal processes. Initially, the life cycle pressure pattern points upwards. But this is only the starting feature of a new learning phase. It is necessarily followed by a long and deep contraction.

In the case of the euro, the pressure pattern is pointing upwards into 2018, but the subsequent fall could last until 2023. Much will therefore depend on the nature of any institutional changes (if any) ahead of the forthcoming trading peak. If the advance is accompanied by a genuine revision of the constituent parts of the euro, then any weakness in 2018–23 will be mild. If, however, the euro's rally further entrenches the political implications of a single currency, then the weakness in 2018–23 will be vicious, because the markets themselves will have to force the necessary structural changes.

# *14*

# The Pattern Of Innovation

## Introduction

THE STANDARD NEO-KEYNESIAN model of economic behaviour assumes an unchanging capital stock. This allows policy-makers to assume that an economic recession is caused by inadequate demand and that therefore a government stimulus is required. The official interventionist model is essentially a short-term one.[117] Over the years, however, this idea has been challenged on the grounds that it ignores supply-side influences. In particular, it has been argued that severe economic stagnation is caused, not by inadequate demand, but by a lack of basic innovations. This was the thesis proposed by Professor Gerhard Mensch in his book *Stalemate in Technology*.[118] It was also an idea pursued by Professor Jacob van Duijn in *The Long Wave in Economic Life*.[119]

The persistence of **deflation** – defined as the combination of economic stagnation and falling prices – since the global financial crisis of 2007–09 brings Professor Mensch's argument back into focus. Indeed, the influence of innovation has recently been reassessed by Professor Robert Gordon, of Northwestern University, who identifies three industrial revolutions in the US.[120] The first (1750–1830) involved steam and rail; the second revolution

---

117   One of Keynes's more famous quotations is that "in the long-run we are all dead". The quotation is a plea for the use of accurate definitions, but is usually misapplied. John M. Keynes, *A Tract On Monetary Reform* (Macmillan & Co Ltd, London, 1923).

118   Gerhard Mensch, *Stalemate in Technology* (Ballinger Publishing Co, Cambridge (Ma.), 1979). Professor Mensch's theory uses the concept of an "S"-shaped growth curve. The value of this curve is discussed in Appendix IV.

119   Jacob van Duijn, *The Long Wave in Economic Life* (George Allen & Unwin, London, 1982).

120   Robert Gordon, *Is US Economic Growth Over?* (National Bureau of Economic Research, Cambridge (Ma,), 2012).

(1870–1900) included electricity, the internal combustion engine, running water, indoor toilets, communications, chemicals, and petroleum; and the third (1960–present) incorporated computers, the World Wide Web, and mobile phones. Professor Gordon maintains that, unlike the second revolution, the third revolution created only a short revival in growth between 1996 and 2004. In addition, he argues that the third revolution is no longer strong enough to stop the US economy from stagnating.

As we shall see, Professor Gordon's classifications differ from those that can be deduced from an innovation-orientated life cycle. They do, however, focus on something that is very important: innovations that are significant to socio-economic evolution are those that make a profound difference to collective living standards.

## Basic innovation

The Life Cycle Hypothesis can be used to track socio-economic change through the lens of new product innovation. The first point to make in this context is that there is a difference between invention and innovation. An invention involves the emergence of a new idea, but there may be a very long time lapse before the idea becomes **practical**. An innovation, on the other hand, is the moment that an invention does actually become practical; it becomes available and is used.

The second point concerns the nature of innovation. Economists distinguish between various **types** of innovation. However, the most important type of innovation involves new **basic** products. Such products can establish new industries (e.g., personal computers and mobile phones), or branches of industry; or they are sufficiently radical to rejuvenate existing industries (e.g., Wi-Fi and camera phones). They create wants, they impart collective optimism, and they boost government tax revenues.[121]

The third point follows from this. There will be associated changes that may support the momentum of change. These include **process** innovations and **artificial** innovations (e.g., new-look hardware and new software). These may be helpful, but they will not revolutionise consumer demand. So, once the impulse from innovation becomes involved with variety rather than with transformation, aggregate demand will begin to tail off. This is when the economy will slip into an irreversible stagnation. Certainly, a Keynesian-type stimulus that involves lower interest rates cannot inspire the introduction of new products.

---

121 It is arguable that this is a very good example of Say's Law, where "supply creates its own demand". Say's Law was discredited by Keynes, so that he could concentrate on the need to boost aggregate demand.

# A look at the data

The phenomenon of innovation is not easy to track. The approach taken by Professor Mensch and Professor van Duijn was to take no account of the quality of a particular innovation, but just to register its arrival. Both researchers therefore summed the arrival of new products onto the market over successive ten-year periods. In this way, the data was able objectively to isolate any clustering of innovations, but it was not able to depict the subjective impact on people's lives.

This methodology leaves the way open for different researchers to argue about the relevance of a particular innovation, and/or to include another innovation that is excluded. Nevertheless, such concerns are subsidiary. The prime objective of Professor Mensch and Professor van Duijn was to produce data sets that: (i) were consistent over time; (ii) tracked the build-up of innovations; and (iii) could isolate breaks in the flow of innovation. The purpose of the data set, therefore, was to identify swings in innovation, rather than the actual numbers of new products.[122]

Gerhard Mensch accordingly constructed an array of innovations starting in the late 18th century and ending in 1950, while Jacob van Duijn built up a data set of innovations stretching from 1811 until 1971. Intriguingly, where the data sets overlap, they are very similar. This allows them to be merged together. Innovations after 1971 were then obtained by searching the internet. The resulting list of innovations stretches from 1795–2009, and it has been reproduced in Appendix III.

In addition, one further adjustment has been made. Professor Mensch and Professor van Duijn used ten-year periods to isolate clusters of innovations. However, in order to focus on the sensitivity of the fluctuations in innovation, the list has here been partitioned into five-year periods, starting from 1795–99 and running through to 2005–09.

# The life cycle

Figure 14-1 reveals the result of this process. The heavy line is the incidence of innovation over successive five-year periods; the dashed line is the evolution-related pressure exerted by the archetypal life cycle pattern.

There are a number of preliminary comments that can be made. Firstly, the relationship between actual innovations and the archetypal pattern is amazingly close. The spikes in the late 1880s, and in the mid-1930s, are particularly clear

---

122   A number of independent researchers have confirmed the presence of broad oscillations in the data. Mensch, *op cit*.

but so, too, are the subsequent discontinuities. Secondly, the life cycle appears to have been triggered into being between 1795 and 1799. Just prior to that time, there must have been something in the environment that generated a creative impulse. Thirdly, as it stands at the moment, the life cycle seems likely to last until around 2055–59. On this basis, the time span of the whole life cycle is about 260 years.

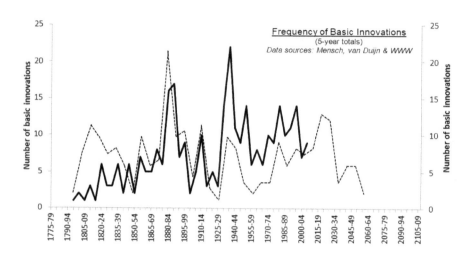

Figure 14-1: Basic innovations and the life cycle

## The Industrial Revolution

This life cycle bears an extremely important relationship to the phenomenon known to historians as the Industrial Revolution. The revolution started in the UK and quickly extended to other countries. It involved the introduction of new technologies and an associated rise in general living standards. The Industrial Revolution was therefore a major turning point in global history. Opinions differ about dates, but the UK's transformation is usually placed in a period dating from around 1760 to somewhere between 1820 and 1840.[123] Against

---

[123] The spinning jenny was introduced into the cotton weaving industry in 1764. The jenny significantly increased the amount of cloth that could be produced by a single worker. It would not have been possible, however, without the flying shuttle, which became available in 1733. The shuttle reduced the number of workers needed to weave a piece of cloth.

this, the archetypal life cycle seems not to have entered the initial stages of a reaction to a creative shock until around 1800. The reaction itself – which is the signal that an evolutionary process has started – lasted for another 20 years or so. Then the absorption stage took over. Figure 14-1 suggests that the whole learning stage (i.e., reaction plus absorption) ended around 1854. It thus took 54 years.

This comparison of the Industrial Revolution with the archetypal life cycle results in an important conclusion. The energies released by the supply-side were themselves the creative shock that generated a socio-economic transformation on the demand-side.

## The learning phase of the life cycle

In many ways, the transition from the 18th century to the 19th century marked the emergence of the modern Western world. The impulse generated by the Industrial Revolution fed through into a demand for new products. The presence of these new products in people's lives represented an improvement in living standards.

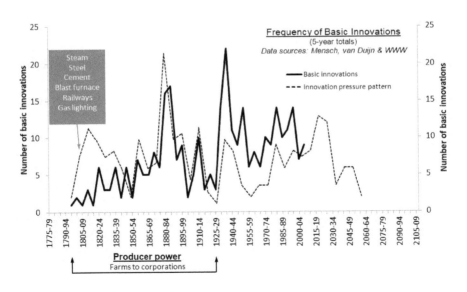

Figure 14-2: The learning phase

Figure 14-2 highlights some of the developments that impacted during the first 54 years of the new life cycle. They are far from being the only achievements in that period, but they emphasise three crucial points. First, the boost to consumer demand from new technologies developed relatively slowly. Second, there had to be a build-up of new interrelated technologies before a new product became effective enough to achieve a significant market penetration. Third, the process of getting used to the idea of change was accompanied by a shift away from an agrarian economy towards new urban-based industries and (therefore) to the influence of powerful individuals. This was, after all, an age typified by Isambard Kingdom Brunel (1806–1859).

## The Threshold Cycle

As indicated in Chapter 3, every learning phase is terminated by a Threshold Cycle. In this case, the cycle ran from the late 1820s to the mid-1850s. Moreover, it followed the standard pattern of an initial advance followed by a fall into an end-cycle low. We can hypothesise that the Threshold Cycle will cement in place the conviction that change is inevitable, but it is often difficult to isolate the events that reflect this conviction.

In this case, it is possible that the inevitability of change was reflected in the work of Isambard Brunel. In 1843, his ship SS Great Britain was launched. It is still regarded as the first modern ship, being made of metal rather than of wood, being powered by an engine rather than by sail, and being driven by a propeller rather than by paddle wheels. Finally, in 1854, Brunel opened Paddington Station as the London terminus of the Great Western Railway. He had designed both.

## The Transition Cycle

Once set in motion, the process of evolution becomes unstoppable. The ending of the Threshold Cycle in or around 1854 therefore triggered the ferocious momentum of the next cycle – the Transition Cycle. According to Figure 14-2, the Transition Cycle ended in the early 1920s. This means that the process of separating cultural beliefs and understandings from the old (i.e., agrarian) world took between 66 and 70 years.

This is a long time for a Transition Cycle to unfold. People do not usually differentiate between slow movement and an unchanging state. Consequently, the movements in a long-duration Transition Cycle have to be violent in order to generate a widespread awareness of change.[124] The 1854–1920/24 innovation-related cycle was no exception. The outstanding feature of the period was

---

[124] Collective awareness/beliefs may not have recognised the presence of ongoing change because the previous learning phase was very extended.

undoubtedly the three-wave swarming of innovations into the 1885–89 peak, followed by an outright collapse into the early years of the 20th century. The former subsequently became known as the Victorian Boom, the latter was experienced (prior to the economic collapse of the 1930s) as a 'great' depression. The result in socio-economic terms was a complete break with the past.

Conventional economists generally have some difficulty explaining these violent swings. In particular, the concept of 'swarming' has raised academic eyebrows.[125] Why should innovations be linked in this way? And yet, in the context of the evolution-related life cycle, the swing from a clustering of innovations (the boom) to an energy gap in risk-taking (the bust) makes sense.

## The upswing of the Transition Cycle

Some of the dominant innovations during the upswing of the Transition Cycle are shown in Figure 14-3. They include the arrival of automobiles and the growth of the petroleum industry; they involve the availability of indoor electric lighting and running water; and they incorporate the start of the communications industry in the form of telephones. These changes impacted people on the individual level and they stimulated the growth of large companies as important sources of employment. This was the era when a significant rise in living standards became available to an increasing number of people.

---

[125] The difficulty in justifying the concept of 'swarming' is one of the main academic criticisms of Gerhard Mensch's work on innovation. However, swarming is perfectly feasible in the context of any form of collective behaviour.

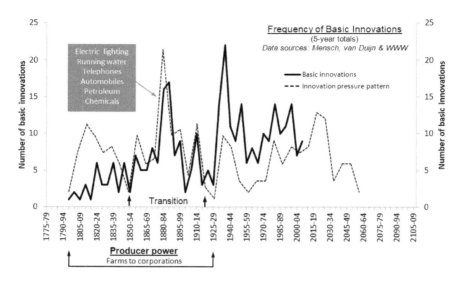

Figure 14-3: The Transition Cycle

## The downswing of the Transition Cycle

The 15-year period after the 1885–89 peak was one of those episodes in history that still eludes adequate interpretation. One moment, the economic environment was booming, the next it had collapsed. We can now see that the implosion in innovation constituted an energy gap within a period of ongoing evolution. In fact, its existence confirmed the operation of a Transition Cycle. This was, however, no consolation for the unemployed, and the period after the 1885–89 peak was accordingly experienced as a 'Great Depression'.

Such implosions are extremely difficult, but they are a natural part of the evolutionary process. Having established the external infrastructure that characterised the Victorian era, the forces of evolution were destined to turn inwards. Queen Victoria herself died in 1901, just as the innovation collapse reached its low. Nevertheless, it still took some time before the innovation life cycle reached its halfway point.

## The second half of the innovation life cycle

The economic and social adjustments after the WWI were sufficiently dramatic to keep the flow of innovation depressed throughout most of the 1920s. The Transformation Cycle itself probably started at the beginning of the 1920s and, like its predecessor, it was destined to last between 66 and 70 years. However, new products were initially slow to materialise, so the innovation life cycle remained weak until its halfway stage.

The dominant feature after the halfway point in the innovation life cycle was a surge in innovation accompanied by an economic collapse. Indeed, the depth of the economic crisis was such that it took over from the economic slump of the late 19th century as being the Great Depression. The synchronicity of these two phenomena is shown in Figure 14-4.

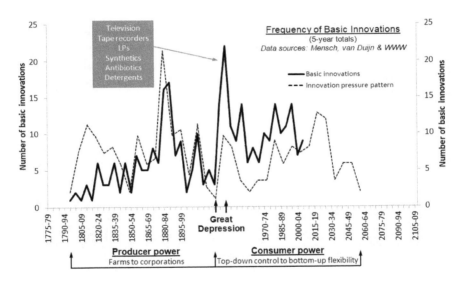

Figure 14-4: The second half of the life cycle

At this stage, it would have been difficult to conclude either that innovation always creates economic growth or that a depression is caused only by a discontinuity in innovation. This has caused some consternation amongst economists. In one sense, the depression was most unusual. As was indicated in Chapter 10, an ordinary slowdown was turned into a disaster by the Federal Reserve's incompetence. This does not, however, explain the surge in innovation during such a psychologically dispiriting period.[126]

---

126  Gerhard Mensch concluded that the depression itself might have encouraged the search for new markets. Gerhard Mensch, *op. cit.*

# Innovation in the 1930s

The conundrum might be explained by the fact that there was something quite distinctive about innovation during the 1930s. Specifically, the 1929–39 innovation cluster was of a different quality to its predecessors. The life cycle pattern suggests that the purpose of this cluster was not to reverse the impact of a prior discontinuity, but to alter the focus of all subsequent change. It was the start of a new learning pattern, and it separated the first half of the cycle from the second half.

The first half of any life cycle creates the container, or structure, for a new form, while the second half fulfils the inner purpose for that form. Prior to 1929, therefore, new infrastructure tended to benefit the whole community; after it, the focus of change shifted towards the individual. This is shown in Figure 14-4. The Great Depression (and the World War that followed) may have helped in their own ways to energise this adjustment. In any case, the second half of the innovation life cycle involved a shift away from producer power towards consumer power.

# The Transformation Cycle

Such a significant shift takes time. The absorption phase of the necessary learning started with the outbreak of the WWII, and probably lasted into the early 1960s. The importance of the ending of the absorption phase cannot be overemphasised. It means that, by the time the phenomenon of the Swinging Sixties came into being, collective psychology was ready for change. The culture itself had learnt – literally – to expect it. Consequently, new products such as television, LPs, and tape recorders were quickly and easily absorbed into the new ethos. Music, art, and different clothing styles became part of the new lifestyle.

Figure 14-5 shows that this trend phase lasted until the late 1980s or early 1990s. As always, the Transformation Cycle ended with a slowdown in the supply of new products but, by that stage, individuals could (if they wished) purchase personal computers, mobile phones, and CD players.

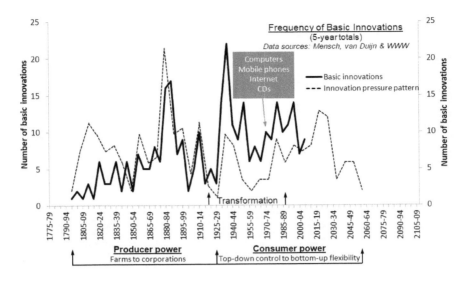

Figure 14-5: The Transformation Cycle

## The Termination Cycle

One of the insights of the Life Cycle Hypothesis is that the Termination Cycle – which is the last of the triad of cycles that drive the processes of evolution – does not involve a major paradigm shift. It is essentially speculative and is connected with finding out what works and what doesn't. In principle, therefore, the Termination Cycle is a period of trial and error. This means that innovation since the early 1990s has largely been built on the developments that preceded it. This doesn't mean that there are no new innovations; it just means that those innovations are unlikely to cause a general upheaval.

It is therefore no great surprise to find that the Termination Cycle has unfolded on the basis of pre-existing ideas. Computers and mobile phones have been smartened to include smaller hand-held units, faster processing speeds, and easier data storage. Access to information, and to retail outlets, has been significantly enhanced by the internet, Wi-Fi, and rapid internet search engines. And, not surprisingly, interpersonal communication via digital technology has exploded. Some of these developments are shown in Figure 14-6. They are not the only ones, but they emphasise the important point that the focus of evolution has undoubtedly shifted even more clearly from the group to the individual.

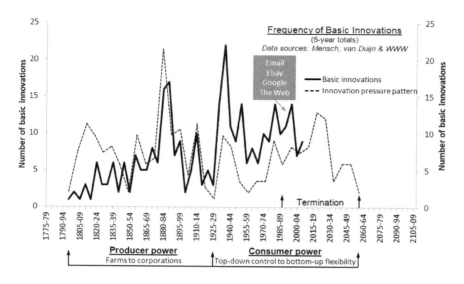

Figure 14-6: Growth of the internet

## Implications

This shift in focus – which in terms of technology has involved a shift away from the manufacture of hardware to the production of software – has altered the potential strength of the economic upswing. As Figure 14-6 shows, the flow of new products contracted in the early years of the 2000s. This weakness was consistent with the underlying shift in the innovation pressure pattern, but its wider implications were quickly picked up by the equity market. As enthusiasm for the digital revolution intensified during the late 1990s, a bubble developed in technology stocks.[127] The downswing in the innovation life cycle was therefore associated with an equity crash. Between March 2000 and October 2002, the technology-based US NASDAQ index fell by almost 80%. Meanwhile, between March 2000 and June 2002, the S&P 500 index lost half its value.

Figure 14-6 clearly shows, however, that this downturn in the innovation cycle is temporary. The upswing of the Termination Cycle should last into the early years of the next decade – that is, until 2020–24. But the sensitivity of the equity markets, and of economic growth, to the innovation cycle now needs to be taken seriously. The period 2024–29 is likely to see a major energy gap, which will be the second (and final) such gap in the innovation cycle that began in the late

---

[127] This is now known as the dot-com bubble.

18th century. This implies that an extremely difficult period may emerge in the very near future. It cannot be just an interesting coincidence that the much shorter 36-year life cycle for business activity – which was analysed in Chapter 9 – is generating a very similar conclusion for the next decade.

## Conclusion

Because of the length of time involved, it is easy to assume that the flow of innovation is constant in order to concentrate on fluctuations in aggregate demand. However, this chapter has shown that innovation is neither unchanging nor simply the framework for collective behaviour. It fluctuates widely – it provides an independent stimulus to behaviour by creating demand, and it therefore contributes to living standards.

It seems that, historically, a supply-side shock triggered demand-side evolution. Specifically, the Industrial Revolution triggered a life cycle in innovation whose upswing could last until around 2020–24. So far, there have been four pronounced clusters of innovation. These occurred in 1800–24, 1870–89, 1929–39, and 1965–99. The clusters of 1800–24 and 1870–89 were each followed by a discontinuity in innovation that either fed into (1840s), or coincided with (1890s), an economic depression. Nevertheless, this is far from being the whole story. The innovation cluster of 1929–39 is not only very marked, it also occurred during the period that is now known as the Great Depression.[128] Moreover, the 1965–99 surge in innovation was followed by a significant slowdown, but that slowdown looks to be only temporary. So it is difficult to conclude either that a depression is caused only by a discontinuity in innovation or that innovation always creates economic growth.

One of the relevant insights is that the flow of innovation has refocused itself away from the group towards the individual. There has therefore been a weakening of national pressures, a separation of the individual away from the whole, and the early stirrings of a process that psychologists call 'individuation'. It is probably an understatement to say that this has huge implications for conventional economic policy, which assumes that aggregate demand can be manipulated to maximise employment and minimise inflation. People will not respond as policy-makers expect. So, the switch away from producing goods for collective needs towards providing services for individual requirements changes the internal dynamics of an economy. Specifically, traditional measures of economic strength will tend to subside – as, eventually, will tax revenues.

128   This particular innovation cluster is ignored by Professor Robert Gordon in his 2012 paper on US economic growth. See Robert Gordon, *op. cit.*

Some of these forces are already apparent. Even so, they do not yet involve an actual discontinuity in innovation. In fact, the final upswing of the life cycle pressure pattern is still ahead. We do not know what additional innovations will be introduced; nor can we know what the consequences will be. But we can flag that a profound challenge will arise when the innovation cycle **does** reach the end of its growth phase. The charts in this chapter suggest that the innovation impulse of a cycle that started in the late 18th century will enter this final discontinuity sometime in the next decade. It will be no small thing!

# 15

# West And East

## Introduction

THIS BOOK HAS outlined the intrinsic pattern of a life cycle and has applied it to a number of phenomena that are driven by collective behaviour. These include the US Dow, 10-year US Treasury Note prices, the euro in terms of the US dollar, US commodity prices, and US output. US data has been used, partly because of the availability of relevant statistics and partly because the US remains central to the global economy. The correlations between the life cycle pattern and the indices being tracked are extraordinary and confirm that collective behaviour is not random.

In addition, the life cycle pattern has been applied both to the average human life and to the flow of innovation. The former applies, in principle, to an individual; the latter tracks new products that enhance living standards. The subjects couldn't be more different: one is obviously a living organism, the other is not. Moreover, neither overtly involves collective behaviour; and both traverse vastly different time periods. In both cases, however, the life cycle pattern was found not only to be applicable, but also to be very precise.

## Anticipating the future

This evidence is sufficiently compelling to shift the burden of proof away from verifying that such a pattern might exist towards the need to demonstrate that it doesn't. Nevertheless, a practical confirmation of the life cycle pattern's existence will necessarily involve an accurate prediction of future developments. To this end, I shall offer two sets of charts. The first is an integrated diagram of three US indices: wholesale prices, output, and 10-year Treasury Notes. In principle, movements in 10-year Treasury Notes should reflect the balance between prices and output.

The second set of charts shows two equity markets: the pattern of behaviour in Japanese equities, as represented by the Nikkei average of 225 stocks; and the emerging patterns in the Chinese equity market, as reflected in the Shanghai Composite Index. These two charts are offered without detailed comment. The idea is to show each equity index within the context of an appropriate life cycle profile. This should give the analyst a clear view about what to expect.

## Expectations for the US

Figure 15-1 shows the profile of potential movements in US wholesale prices, industrial production, and 10-year Treasury Note prices. All three chart lines are taken directly from the life cycle profiles that were demonstrated in earlier chapters. The black dashed line is the profile for wholesale prices. It includes both the learning phase that evolved after the global financial crisis and the anticipated Transition Cycle (see Chapter 12). The heavy black line is the pattern for US industrial production. It shows how the Transition Cycle that began in late 2015 can be expected to unfold (see Chapter 9). Finally, the grey dashed line is the likely profile for US Treasury Note prices. It shows how the Termination Cycle that started in December 2013 and January 2014 can be expected to develop (see Chapter 11).

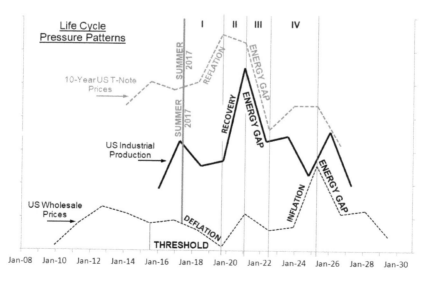

Figure 15-1: Future conditions in the US

In principle, the 10-year Treasury Note index should reflect the balance of pressures between cost inflation and business activity. Consequently, placing the three chart lines together in this way reveals how different aspects of the US economy can be expected to evolve in the years ahead. The vertical grey line shows the approximate starting point in summer 2017. All future developments will therefore unfold to the right of this line. It will, however, be important to remember that these developments will reflect the balance between life cycle pressures and contemporaneous events. They cannot be absolutely precise.

## The implications: Phase I

The first point to note is the logicality of the relationships between the three lines. In order to make this clearer, I have divided the developments between summer 2017 and mid-2025 into four phases (I to IV). The diagram suggests that the US economy is entering Phase I. During this phase, wholesale prices look likely to weaken and the growth of US output should start to moderate. Faced with these conditions the US authorities are likely to reflate (insofar as they are able) by reducing interest rates. 10-year Treasury Note prices could therefore rise sharply. As of summer 2017, it seems premature to call for a major bear in US bond prices.

## Phase II

Phase II could last from late 2019 to early 2021. It represents the response to the reflation of Phase I. The stimulus should initiate an economic recovery and encourage a rise in wholesale prices. Economic conditions in summer 2017 are not the same as they were just after the financial crisis in 2009. Consequently, any economic recovery should be more robust. At this stage, US Treasury Notes should begin to fall in price terms.

## Phase III

Phase III could last from early 2021 to mid-2022. The inflation pressures of Phase II will probably already have underlined the seriousness of what is happening. Phase III will be characterised by an energy gap in Treasury Note prices. The point is that the behaviour of Treasury Note prices after January 2014 belongs to that market's **Termination** Cycle. The energy gap during this cycle is the **final** energy gap within an evolutionary process that started in 1977. So, once the Termination Cycle has reached its peak and turns down, there is likely to be a full trend reversal in Treasury Note prices.

Such a breakdown would impact the business sector. As bond prices fall and yields surge, output should drop sharply. In fact, output is likely to enter its own energy gap. This would be the first such gap of the new 36-year era that began in late 2015. Wholesale price inflation should be suppressed, but the cost would be a shocking recession.

## Phase IV

The diagram indicates that the problem is likely to revolve around an increase in inflation expectations. This may be the primary issue for the period from mid-2022 until the inflation peak in 2024–27. Hence, as the process shifts into Phase IV, wholesale price inflation should pick up sharply. We don't yet know what might cause this surge; nor do we know precisely when it might end. It could be monetary and credit reflation, it could be a climatic shock, or it could be an armed conflict.[129] In any case, inflation pressures would be a major burden for general business activity. At this stage, the effects on the Treasury market would probably depend both on how far Treasury Note prices have fallen in Phase III, and on the emerging balance between weak output and rising inflation.

# Inferences

With conventional tools, the longer the time horizon that is used, the less compelling become the forecasts. Small input errors in the early years can cause large output discrepancies at later dates. This is not necessarily true with the Life Cycle Hypothesis. If we allow some variability in the timing of turning points, and concentrate on the direction of movement rather than on the final location of that movement, then potential outcomes become focused.

This is likely to be true for the US between late 2019 and the early years of the next decade. The Life Cycle Hypothesis suggests that conditions will be traumatic, involving an energy gap in business activity, an energy gap in Treasury Note prices, and a surge in inflation.

In addition, the interaction of the life cycle profiles for different variables can either isolate inconsistencies or reveal new information about developing trends. In particular, knowing which particular phase of a life cycle is relevant can determine how it should be interpreted. The after-effects of a crash during a Transition Cycle, for example, are significantly different to the after-effects of the learning phase during a Transformation Cycle. And both are different in nature to the effects of the advancing stage of a Termination Cycle.

---

[129] See Chapter 12.

# Japanese equities

The importance of knowing the status of an evolutionary life cycle can be emphasised by reference to other indices. Figure 15-2 shows the status of the Japanese equity market, as tracked by the Nikkei. The heavy black line shows the Nikkei itself; the thin black line shows the two-year momentum of that index; the black dashed line is the proposed life cycle pressure pattern; and the grey dashed line is the momentum of that pressure pattern.

The immense bubble from 1982–1989, and then the crash between 1989 and 1992, are almost self-evident. It is important to remember that the bubble itself genuinely anticipates an optimistic future, while the crash starts to reorientate resources and attitudes towards that future.[130] A bubble-and-crash confirms the presence of a Transition Cycle.

As presented, the Transition Cycle started in December 1977 and ended in September 2001. It therefore lasted almost 24 years. This suggests that the whole life cycle probably sprang into being in 1959 and that it will end in 2049. Its duration is thus 90 years.[131]

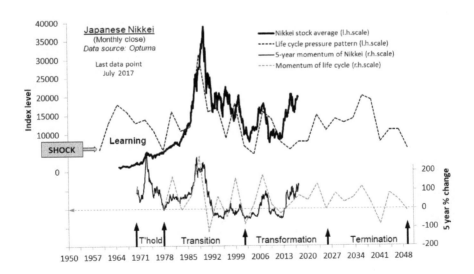

Figure 15-2: Japanese equities

---

130  This is one of the inferences for the US that can be drawn from the combined phenomenon of the 'Roaring Twenties' and the Wall Street Crash.
131  See Appendix I for the importance of this number.

This interpretation means that the 2002–07 advance started during the second half of the life cycle. Specifically, it was the initial part of the new learning phase. The subsequent absorption phase – which involved another collapse in the Nikkei – then lasted until May 2012. The direct inference is that the Japanese equity market is now in the trend phase of the Transformation Cycle. This helps to explain its ongoing strength since 2012.

There are grounds for supposing that the market is approaching a temporary slowdown. This means that more conventional technical and economic indicators can be used to track the Nikkei's performance.[132] Nevertheless, the advance in the Transformation Cycle is not due to end until around 2023.

## Chinese equities

Figure 15-3 shows Chinese equities, as tracked by the Shanghai Composite Index (SCI). The heavy black line shows the SCI itself; the thin black line shows the two-year momentum of that index; the black dashed line is the proposed life cycle pressure pattern; and the grey dashed line is the momentum of that pressure pattern.

The equity crash of 2007–08 is very evident, and its presence indicates the influence of a Transition Cycle. This in itself is important information. So, following the crash event within the Transition Cycle, there has been an inevitable three-phase recovery. The high of that recovery arrived in mid-2015 and, since then, the SCI has been in a natural falling phase. As of summer 2017, this weakness may still be unfinished. In other words, further falls are possible. This is a warning.

The SCI's Transition Cycle will probably end before the end of 2017 but, in the meantime, the length of that cycle will remain uncertain. Consequently, any estimate of the duration of the whole life cycle will have to be flexible. Figure 15-3 suggests that the life cycle started in 1984/85 and will finish in 2056/57. This indicates an overall duration of 71 to 73 years.[133]

The Transformation Cycle can only start when the Transition Cycle has finished. Even after this has happened, however, the SCI will not immediately enter the second half of the whole cycle. So there could still be some uncertainty about the strength of the SCI until late 2018 or early 2019. The only certain indicator

---

[132] One of the relevant indicators is a 38.2% retracement of the 1989–2012 bear. This forms a boundary beyond which fundamentals (whatever they may be) will change. The importance of the golden ratio, 38.2:61.8, is presented in Appendix II.

[133] See Appendix I for the intrinsic importance of these numbers.

that a Transformation Cycle has properly begun will be evidence of a genuine inflexion.[134]

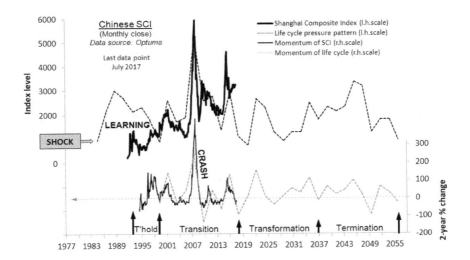

Figure 15-3: Chinese equities

The learning phase of the second half of the life cycle begins after the halfway mark. This phase will be associated with new understandings or beliefs, and it could last eight to ten years. So it will be important to look behind the actual movements in the SCI to gauge the impact of evolution. Once the learning phase has finished, a genuine, and sustainable, trend in the SCI will emerge.

## Conclusion

The idea that evolution is an ordered process has profound implications for our understandings of collective behaviour, both in the economic sphere and in financial market speculation. This chapter has shown that it is entirely possible to know where we are in a longer-term process and to anticipate the future based on that process. This does not mean that the predictions will be either faultless or accurate in terms of detail; but they will undoubtedly reduce the degree of uncertainty that normally emerges when we face the future.

---

134   The signal for a full advance includes considerations relating to the golden ratio, 38.2:61.8. See Appendix II.

Given the dangers that seem likely to confront the US in the early part of the next decade, the behavioural profiles of the Japanese Nikkei and the Chinese SCI are very revealing. The Nikkei is in a Transformation Cycle, and the SCI is finishing a Transition Cycle. This means that the longer-term outlook for both markets is now relatively positive. This does not, of course, mean that they will be able to avoid the trauma that seems set to impact the US economy and related markets in the early years of the next decade. But it does confirm that a switch in global dominance – from West to East – is already in process. Moreover, that switch is part of evolution; as such, it is irreversible.

# *16*

# A Summing Up

## Introduction

I N 1927 WILLIAM Delbert Gann released his book, *Tunnel Thru The Air*. Concealed in the structure of that book was a pattern of vibration that has the power to change the way that we look at the world. The pattern directs the processes of evolution in every living organism from the moment of its creation to the moment of its death. The extraordinary fact is that the pattern also applies to diverse phenomena such as financial market speculation and business activity. The inference is that collective behaviour can itself be treated as a living organism.

The pattern is that of a dynamic life cycle. It has a beginning and an end, and it tracks the rhythm of evolution. The life cycle is not, however, a predetermined path along which an organism will tread; it represents, instead, the pressures to which an organism will respond. Even so, the pattern itself is not random; in fact, its locus is very precise. An externally-generated shock triggers a process of learning. This, in turn, produces a three-phase oscillation that applies those learnings, develops them, and then filters the results. It seems that shocks are essential to genuine evolution; seemingly abnormal developments are actually part of a normal process.

Every new life cycle pattern emerges in the context of a holding field. This emphasises the hierarchical – and closely integrated – nature of life as we understand it. The pattern is ubiquitous, and therefore links phenomena that might otherwise be considered separate. And the pattern is universal, which points to the existence of laws of life that are not currently recognised.

## Learning from a creative shock

The initial response to a creative shock from an organism will take the form of a simple reaction. This will change very little within the organism itself. Instead, the organism is taken to the limit of its abilities. Inevitably, however, once the organism has perceived (in whatever way is appropriate) that the change in the environment is irreversible, it has to adjust its inner variables (or memory). This adjustment can be seen as shifting the contents of short-term memory into long-term memory. I have called this particular phase of the learning process the 'absorption' phase.

The intriguing aspect of the absorption phase is that it will normally end with an explicit confirmation that the organism has learnt that a permanent change in the environment has occurred, and that further changes can now be accommodated. My research suggests that there may be a short space of time where the organism falsely assumes that some form of normality has been achieved and that no further inner changes are necessary. This mismatch between presumption and reality can result in disappointment for a sentient being and despair in collective sentiment. It certainly generates an intensification of the absorption process. I have called this particular phase the Threshold Cycle.

## Three aspects of evolution

Once an organism has learnt that a change has occurred in its environment (or context), and adjusted itself so that it is ready to evolve, then actual evolution can take place. Mr Gann's hidden pattern suggests that this evolution will unfold naturally through three distinctive oscillations. Moreover, the three oscillations will have a similar duration.

Although the ideas have a general application, I shall here confine myself to their relevance to economic activity and to behaviour in financial markets. One important insight, therefore, is that collective behaviour has the same general characteristics as a physical organism. Crowds and groups are held together by common beliefs and attitudes. This was a theme that I developed in the various editions of *Forecasting Financial Markets*.[135]

### The Transition Cycle

The first oscillation I have called a Transition Cycle. This separates the evolving structure from the constraints of its history. In order to achieve this separation, the Transition Cycle is inherently violent. In financial markets, a Transition Cycle will incorporate a bubble-and-crash. The crash is an energy gap within the

---

[135] See Tony Plummer, *Forecasting Financial Markets* (Kogan Page, London, 1989–2010).

process of evolution. It marks the end of the quantitative growth stage of any new organism and sets up a process that shifts the focus of attention towards quality. In this sense, a financial crash is not just the end of the bubble, but is also the start of something new.

## The Transformation Cycle

The second oscillation I have called a Transformation Cycle. This is where the new infrastructure (physical and intellectual) will get laid down. It will normally start, after a lag, with a new learning phase. This helps to shift the focus of evolution away from quantitative change towards qualitative change. This is therefore the period when genuine innovation is important. In financial markets, the Transformation Cycle is the one that is most clearly associated with a trend move. Inevitably, the momentum of this trend will create excesses. These will have to be unwound as the cycle ends.

## The Termination Cycle

The third oscillation I have called a Termination Cycle. This is a cycle whose upswing is based on testing the limits of the new environment, but whose downswing is generated by the resulting excesses. It is thus a trial and error period. The cycle may include further innovations, but the important point is that it is no longer driven by them. It is essentially speculative. Consequently, speculative excesses will eventually trigger an energy gap. This is the second such gap after that generated during the Transition Cycle. Just like its predecessor, the energy gap in the Termination Cycle starts a process of adjustment. In this case, however, the adjustment is towards the death of whatever it is that constitutes the organism.

# Conclusion

This book has presented the idea that evolution is driven, not by wholly random forces, but by an ordered process that is initiated by shocks devolved from a higher level. The fact that we cannot see the source of the shocks – and that they appear random – does not mean that they emerge from nowhere. A valid starting point is that we simply do not understand the higher-order objectives of evolution.

A creative shock generates a sequence of changes that unfolds in an ordered manner through time. The shock is new information – a change that makes a change – and the resulting process may be viewed either as a new system within an existing organism, or as the formation of a new organism.[136] In either case, the response itself must have some form of memory upon which the new system or organism can build. All that is necessary is that the responding system learns that the change in its context/environment is permanent.

Mr Gann's pressure pattern indicates that the evolutionary response of a living system to a creative shock is driven through a triad of oscillations. Each of these contains a significant intra-cycle setback and, of these, the first and third are potentially traumatic. These setbacks are energy gaps: the first helps to switch the focus of evolution from outer structure to inner process; the second switches the focus of change from development to disappearance.

I have taken the liberty of deconstructing Mr Gann's pattern to make it applicable to the modern world. I do not know whether Mr Gann himself was aware of the extraordinary nature of the pattern, but there should be no doubt that, without him, we would not know about it.

---

[136]   In truth, the difference relates to the nature of the holding field; it is a matter of perspective. In the case of change within an existing organism, the holding field is the organism itself; in the case of a new organism, the holding field is the environment in which that organism gestates.

# *Appendix I*

## The Circle Of Nines

### Introduction

I have for many years believed that Mr Gann knew far more than he ever admitted. Moreover, I suspect that his teachings – although effective in themselves – were partially designed to cover up some of his esoteric knowledge. We can only speculate on why this was so, but, if we can uncover some of his knowledge, we will be taking a large step towards changing humanity's view both of itself and of its purpose in the universe.

### The Square of Nine

One of Mr Gann's tools is known as the Square of Nine. It consists of a sequence of numbers, each being one unit higher than its predecessor, which starts either from unity or zero. In the basic form of the Square of Nine, successive numbers are placed in a square in such a way that they rotate around the starting number. Each time a sequence of numbers completes a square, the next number starts a new square. The result has been described as two-dimensional mapping of a three-dimensional pyramidal number form.[137] An example of the procedure is shown in Figure AI-1.

In the diagram, four lines are drawn: a cardinal cross that runs from North to South and from West to East, and two diagonals that run from North West to South East and from North East to South West. The diagonal lines will also intersect with the corners of each number square.

The squaring process then starts with '1' (or '0') at the centre. It doesn't matter which way the diagram rotates. In Figure AI-1, the rotation is counter-clockwise.

---

137    Trevor Casey, *The Square Spiral* (BookPal, Queensland, Australia, 2010).

Hence, one square to the right becomes (1 + 1 =) '2'; the next square up becomes (2 + 1 =) '3'; the next square to the left becomes (3 + 1 =) '4'... etc. Each time a number meets a diagonal, the next number changes direction. In this way, the number sequence spirals around the centre. The first square within the spiral ends on the number '9', so the diagram is called the Square of Nine. In theory, however, the process will continue into infinity.

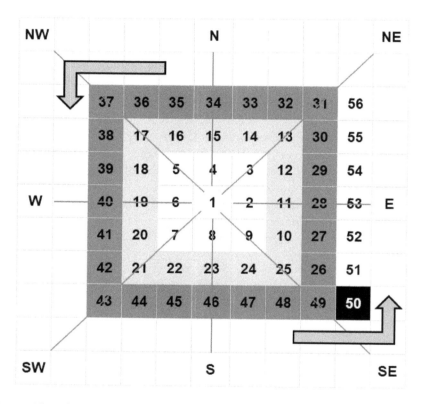

Figure AI-1: The Square of Nine

The importance of the diagram is that it is supposed to indicate potential turning points, measured in time units, in financial markets. Each of the lines linking the centre of the square with one of the eight major compass bearings runs through a set of numbers. Any one of these numbers could be a turning point. Hence, whenever the time lapse from a prior market inflexion reaches one of the lines, then the market is vulnerable to a change in direction.

In Figure AI-1, for example, an equity market might reverse direction at 40 units of time from a prior turning point or at 43 units of time from that turning point. This process could be applied to more than one of the previous highs and lows. An analyst would then be looking for a moment in time where this resulted in a cluster of time intervals.

## The Circle of Nines

Many analysts use the Square of Nine diagram with a great deal of success. However, either it may have been one of Mr Gann's smoke screens or it may have been just one method of calculating time targets from amongst a larger set. There is, in fact, another diagram that uses the number 9 and that is also based on a spiral. This is the Circle of Nines.[138]

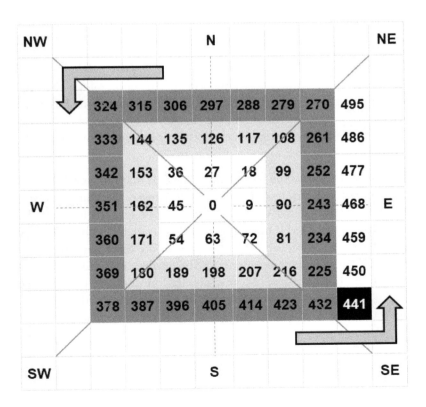

Figure AI-2: Circle of Nines

[138] Mr Gann may have used 'Square' instead of 'Circle', and diverted attention from a multitude of 'Nines' by focusing on a single 'Nine'.

This particular diagram is constructed by the same process as the Square of Nine. However, the centre always starts at zero (which in this context is indistinguishable from infinity); each successive number in the sequence is 9 higher than its predecessor; and all of the digits in every number in the diagram sum to '9'.[139] Consequently, the spiral widens out through the number series 0, 9, 18, 27, 36, 45, 54, 63, 72, … etc. The process is shown in Figure AI-2. In theory, the series can extend to infinity but, in the diagram, only the first three circles around the centre are included.

As with the Square of Nine, the lines linking the centre with the eight main directional bearings register the time units that could trigger a market reversal or cycle inflexion. Moreover, there is some flexibility in the use of the relevant numbers. It may be that the important numbers are not just those on a line, but also the numbers on either side of the line. This means that there is a range that can be applied. Importantly, this range narrows as the diagram moves into higher numbers. In this sense, the Circle of Nines may even become more accurate at higher numbers.

## Precession of the Equinoxes

The importance of the number 9 is that, in ancient numerology, that number is known as the 'number of completion'. A given sequence would be considered to have ended once it reached a number that could be reduced to the number '9'.[140] This sort of thinking would have been very important to Mr Gann, who was particularly interested in ancient numerology.

The first point to make about the Circle of Nines is that some of the important numbers relate to vibrations of the universe. Of these, two stand out: the first is the number 26,001; and the second is the number 432. The former (which is not shown in Figure AI-2) is the number that is associated with the **Precession of the Equinoxes**,[141] whereby the vertical axis of the Earth oscillates slowly in a cycle of approximately 26,000 years.[142] The result is that the location of the pole star shifts through time. Meanwhile, the number 432 (which is in the third circuit in Figure AI-2) is the number that is associated with a Pythagorean tuning of the note 'A' to 432 Hz instead of to the conventional 440 Hz.

---

[139]   For example, in Figure AI-2, the number '216' reduces to 2 + 1 + 6 = 9.
[140]   See note 139.
[141]   The Precession of the Equinoxes is usually measured in relation to the spring equinox, where the length of the night is equal to the length of the day. Each year, the rising sun will have 'precessed' – i.e., travelled anti-clockwise – in relation to the background zodiac.
[142]   The length of the cycle is currently about 25,920 years in duration. The rising sun will therefore exit one sign of the zodiac and enter another every 2,160 years or so. The number 216 is one of the important numbers on the Circle of Nines.

The digits in the number 26,001, when added together, equal 9 (i.e., 2 + 6 + 0 + 0 + 1 = 9). The same, of course, applies to the number 432 (i.e., 4 + 3 + 2 = 9). There does seem to be something important about the number '9' in the context of movement within the universe.

## Doubling and halving sequences

Secondly, the initial circuit around the centre indicates the presence of a doubling sequence: 18 is double 9; 36 is double 18; and 72 is double 36. Thus, for example, Professor Brian Berry has been able to find pairs of 'mode-locked' nine-year business cycles within a larger 18-year cycle.[143] And it is well known that Mr Gann considered that doubling was an important element in the advance of financial markets. The 2002–07 rise in the S&P 500, for example, amounted to just over a doubling.

By definition, of course, this means that halvings are also important. One of the most important downside barriers for a falling market is an absolute fall of 50%. The 2000–02 fall in the S&P 500, for example, amounted to 50%.

There is, however, a difference between a doubling and a halving. There is a lower bound to the halving process that is not mirrored in an upper bound to doubling. Ultimately, there is a limit to the extent to which a market can fall, but (in theory anyway) there is no upper limit on a market's ability to rise.

## Collective behaviour

Thirdly, the Circle of Nines diagram obviously holds numbers that can be found in collective behaviour. The initial circuit, for example, includes the numbers 36, 54, and 72. In Chapter 9, we saw that the number 36 is particularly relevant to cycles in output; in Chapter 12, we saw that the number 54 dominates the cycles in price movements; and in Chapter 15, we saw that the number 72 might apply to the Chinese equity market. There are, of course, other numbers that are relevant. The second circuit, for example, contains the number 90, which references the duration of the life cycle in the Japanese Nikkei that was analysed in Chapter 15.

# Conclusion

There are no certainties when it comes to isolating numbers that might somehow be embedded in the evolution of the universe. Nevertheless, it is quite clear that the diagram known as the Circle of Nines holds important information

---

143 Brian J. L. Berry, 'A Pacemaker for the Long Wave', in *Technological Forecasting and Social Change* (Elsevier, 2000).

that may relate to the passage of time in business cycles and in financial market speculation. This does not mean that than Mr Gann's more well-known Square of Nine is irrelevant, but it may mean that closer attention needs to be paid to alternatives.

# *Appendix II*

## Critical Ratios

## Introduction

In *The Law of Vibration*, I argued that William Gann had used a very specific idea in his approach to support and resistance in financial markets. He considered that market movements could be interrupted at key levels that were defined by the musical octave. This does not mean that financial markets are driven by the musical octave itself, but that the forces that have created that octave are the same forces that influence financial markets. This is why the two phenomena are correlated.

There are, therefore, three important points: firstly, each octave contains three inner octaves; secondly, each inner octave terminates at a doubling on the way up, or on a halving on the way down; and, thirdly, critical boundaries within any process of change can be found at levels in an octave defined by the golden ratio, 38.2:61.8.

## Support and resistance

Table AII-1 shows an eight note octave starting with a DO that vibrates at 128 cycles per second and that ends with a DO that vibrates at 2048 cycles per second. Obviously, this particular version of the octave has been chosen so that it can used to demonstrate some of the relevant ideas.

The overall octave (i.e., the outer octave) starts from a DO. This is assumed to set in motion a process, rather than being part of that process. For simplicity, this initiating DO has here been called DO$^{LO}$. The process consists of three inner octaves, which stretch sequentially from RE to MI, from MI to SO, and from SO to DO$^{HI}$. Each of these inner octaves represents a doubling in vibrations.

In terms of duration, therefore, the striking of the DO$^{LO}$ note corresponds to the creative shock, while the sounding of that note then corresponds to the learnings from that shock. The three inner octaves correspond to the three oscillations in the life cycle (i.e., the Transition Cycle, the Transformation Cycle, and the Termination Cycle, respectively). It is an extraordinary fact that the equal lengths of the inner octaves (i.e., as measured by the three doublings in vibration between RE and DO$^{HI}$ in the outer octave) are reflected in the equal lengths of the life cycle oscillations.

| Outer | | Inner | | | Inner vibration as % of total inner vibrations |
|---|---|---|---|---|---|
| Note | Vibration | Note | Vibration | Difference from previous lower | |
| DO$^{HI}$ | 2048 | Do | 2048.0 | 128.0 | 100.00 |
| | | Ti | 1920.0 | 213.3 | 92.86 |
| TI | 1792 | | | | |
| | | La | 1706.7 | 170.7 | **80.95** |
| | | So | 1536.0 | 170.7 | 71.43 |
| LA | 1365 | Fa | 1365.3 | 85.3 | 61.90 |
| | | Me | 1280.0 | 128.0 | 57.14 |
| | | Re | 1152.0 | 128.0 | 50.00 |
| SO | 1024 | Do | 1024.0 | 64.0 | 42.86 |
| | | Ti | 960.0 | 106.7 | **39.29** |
| | | La | 853.3 | 85.3 | 33.33 |
| | | So | 768.0 | 85.3 | 28.57 |
| FA | 683 | Fa | 682.7 | 42.7 | 23.81 |
| | | Me | 640.0 | 64.0 | 21.43 |
| | | Re | 576.0 | 64.0 | 17.86 |
| ME | 512 | Do | 512.0 | 32.0 | 14.29 |
| | | Ti | 480.0 | 53.3 | 12.50 |
| | | La | 426.7 | 42.7 | 9.52 |
| | | So | 384.0 | 42.6 | 7.14 |
| | | Fa | 341.4 | 21.4 | 4.77 |
| | | Me | 320.0 | 32.0 | 3.57 |
| | | Re | 288.0 | 32.0 | 1.79 |
| RE | 256 | Do | 256.0 | 0.0 | 0.00 |
| DO$^{LO}$ | 128 | | | | |

Table AII-1: The musical octave

The idea of an outer octave that consists of three inner octaves can also be applied to the price dimension. The basic idea is that, in a rising market, there will be resistance either on a doubling from a previous low or at an interval calculated in relation to the price span of a prior fall. In a falling market, there will be support at a halving, or at an interval calculated in relation to the price span of a previous rise. I have analysed this in some detail in *The Law of Vibration*, and will not repeat the exercise here. Far more important in the current context are the levels indicated by the golden ratio.

## Jumping the gap

The sixth column in Table AII-1 shows two highlighted numbers. All the numbers in the column are ratios, derived by dividing the cumulative rise in vibration of the relevant inner ratio by the increase in vibration covered by all three inner octaves (i.e., the increase in vibration from RE to DO^HI) and then multiplying the result by 100. The highlighted numbers reflect some form of interruption to the process of ascending the musical scale.

Table AII-1 also shows the difference between the vibration of a note and the vibration of the previous note. In most cases, there is an acceleration in the rate of ascent. This signifies a degree of strength. However, in each of the inner octaves, there are slowdowns in the rate of ascent between ME and FA and between TI and DO. These slowdowns correspond to *energy gaps* in the circuit around the enneagram that I described in Chapter 2. They therefore correspond to the position of potential corrections during a market advance.

The inference is that a market advance will reach the second inner TI with some degree of strength, but will then be faced with an energy gap across which it must jump in order to reach the next inner DO. In other words, to reach outer SO an inner gap has to be jumped.

The sixth column shows that the vibration of the second inner TI corresponds to 39.3% of the total difference in vibrations between outer RE and outer DO^HI. If we therefore assume that the previous fall in the market entailed a drop from outer DO^HI to outer RE, and that this drop can be represented by unity, then 39.3% relates to the advance from the market low relative to the prior bear. In other words, at around a 39.3% retracement of the prior fall, a market will face a decision – either it will encounter resistance and drop back, or it will break through it and continue on upwards. In the latter case, a jump across the gap means that a new DO will come into effect and act as a stimulus.

# The link

This is an extraordinary insight into the nature of financial markets. It means that there is a retracement boundary that differentiates a recovery within an ongoing downtrend from a reversal in the trend itself. An example is shown in Figure AII-1. A 39.3% retracement of the whole 2000–02 bear is 9,039.20. After touching its final low in October 2002, the DJIA recovered to 9,076.35, and then fell back.[144] The 39.3% retracement boundary had acted as a barrier. It wasn't until after the market had broken up through that barrier in mid-2003 that equities began to move into a genuine bull advance.

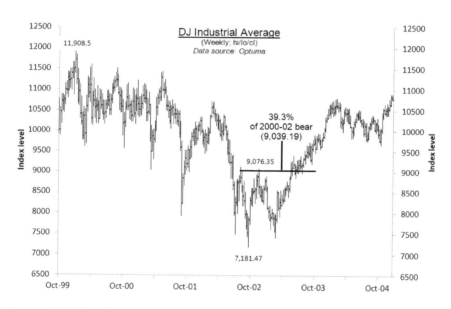

Figure AII-1: The 39.3% retracement boundary

There is an important point here. Trend movements in a financial market are dependent on the underlying trend in fundamentals. Consequently a break upwards beyond the 39.3% retracement boundary must automatically imply a change in the fundamentals. Only then can the market lock into positive feedback with a changing environment.

---

[144] The 39.3% retracement boundary coincided with historical resistance dating from August 2002.

# The golden ratio

In practical terms, the ratio 39.3% is very close to 38.2%, which is one aspect of the golden ratio, 38.2:61.8. Figure AII-2, for example, shows that the 2000–02 bear phase in the DJIA was followed by a recovery. A 38.2% retracement of the bear indicated resistance at an index level of 8,987.20. This level was only marginally different to that calculated using the ratio 39.3%, and the DJIA went through it in mid-2003.

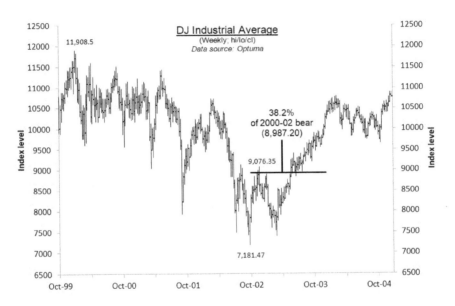

Figure AII-2: The DJIA, 1999–2004

As we shall see below, the ratio 38.2% is particularly important in calculating retracements during an advance. It is therefore possible to use the ratio 38.2% as a critical boundary whether the market is rising or falling. The basic rule is that the 38.2% retracement ratio is the boundary between a correction within an ongoing trend and a reversal in the trend itself. This translates into saying that a market will retain 61.8% of its trend unless there is some reason for that trend to change. Almost invariably, the trend change will involve a change in fundamentals. In my opinion, the golden ratio is the link between market fluctuations and genuine fundamentals.

## The importance of 81%

The other ratio that is highlighted in the sixth column of Table AII-1 is 81%. It is apparent from the table that to get from the third inner LA to the third inner TI in a rising market, it will be necessary to cross beyond the outer TI. And there will be a huge energy gap between outer TI and outer DO$^{HI}$. In practical terms, this means that a full retracement of a prior bear can run into severe difficulties after an advance has covered 81% of that bear. It is as if there is very little difference between an 81% retracement and a 100% retracement.

One inference is that, if a market does retrace more than 81% of a bear, then it will probably retrace the whole of that bear.

## Descending markets

The importance of the 38.2% retracement boundary becomes very clear during a correction within an ongoing bull advance. Indeed, if anything, the ratio is more accurate than during a reversal into a rising market. However, it is not the only important retracement.

Table AII-2 shows the relevant calculations. The fifth column shows the changes in vibration as a market falls. The seventh column shows the cumulative drop in vibration as a percentage of the total increase in vibrations during a bull advance. Two of these percentages are highlighted – i.e., 38.1% and 50.0%.

| Outer | | Inner | | | | |
|---|---|---|---|---|---|---|
| Note | Vibration | Note | Vibration | Difference from previous higher | Inner vibration as % of total inner vibrations | Retracements during fall |
| DO^HI | 2048 | Do | 2048.0 | 0.0 | 100.00 | 0.00 |
| | | Ti | 1920.0 | −128.0 | 92.86 | 7.14 |
| TI | 1792 | | | | | |
| | | La | 1706.7 | −213.3 | **80.95** | 19.05 |
| | | So | 1536.0 | −170.7 | 71.43 | 28.57 |
| LA | 1365 | Fa | 1365.3 | −170.7 | 61.90 | **38.10** |
| | | Me | 1280.0 | −85.3 | 57.14 | 42.86 |
| | | Re | 1152.0 | −128.0 | 50.00 | **50.00** |
| SO | 1024 | Do | 1024.0 | −128.0 | 42.86 | 57.14 |
| | | Ti | 960.0 | −64.0 | **39.29** | 60.71 |
| | | La | 853.3 | −106.7 | 33.33 | 66.67 |
| | | So | 768.0 | −85.3 | 28.57 | 71.43 |
| FA | 683 | Fa | 682.7 | −85.3 | 23.81 | 76.19 |
| | | Me | 640.0 | −42.7 | 21.43 | 78.57 |
| | | Re | 576.0 | −64.0 | 17.86 | 82.14 |
| ME | 512 | Do | 512.0 | −64.0 | 14.29 | 85.71 |
| | | Ti | 480.0 | −32.0 | 12.50 | 87.50 |
| | | La | 426.7 | −53.3 | 9.52 | 90.48 |
| | | So | 384.0 | −42.7 | 7.14 | 92.86 |
| | | Fa | 341.4 | −42.6 | 4.77 | 95.23 |
| | | Me | 320.0 | −21.4 | 3.57 | 96.43 |
| | | Re | 288.0 | −32.0 | 1.79 | 98.21 |
| RE | 256 | Do | 256.0 | −32.0 | 0.00 | 100.00 |
| DO^LO | 128 | | | | | |

Table AII-2: Retracements in a falling market

The ratio 38.1% is a direct reference to 38.2%. As the fifth column shows, to fall beyond 38.1%/38.2%, the market would have to negotiate a drop in vibration. In other words, it would have to negotiate an energy gap. In practical terms, this means that the ratio forms a boundary beyond which influences on the market would have to change. The ratio 38.2% is thus the limit of a fall within the context of a correction.

Figure AII-3 shows two examples of the operation of the 38.2% downside boundary during the bull advance in the DJIA after the global financial crisis. Firstly, the May–October 2011 fall retraced 38.2% of the rise between March 2009 and May 2011; and, secondly, the April–August 2015 fall retraced 38.2% of the rise between October 2011 and April 2015.[145]

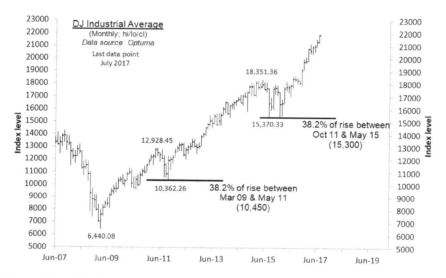

Figure AII-3: 38.2% retracement boundaries

## 50% retracements

But what if the market drops through a 38.2% downside boundary? In this case, a 50% retracement is relevant and important. Mr Gann's techniques already make clear that a halving is of crucial importance because it means a fall through an octave. Here, however, the forces at work become clearer. The 50% boundary relates not to the whole inner octave, but to the first seven notes of that inner octave. The new piece of information, therefore, is that if the market retraces more than 50% of an upswing, it automatically finishes one octave and enters a lower one. On this basis, the 50% retracement boundary becomes very important. Below it, the market could retrace the whole of any previous rise.

---

[145] Elliott Wave practitioners may see the presence of a five-wave pattern in Figure AII-3.

## Qualifications

There are two qualifications to this analysis. The first is that there is always going to be a degree of randomness involved in the area of the relevant retracement boundary. So the market may actually drop through it temporarily. Sometimes, the market will use a boundary as a centre of gravity for short-term oscillations.

The second qualification is that the whole analysis can be conducted in relation to a base of zero. This means that the ratios 38.2%, 50%, and 81% can refer to the extent of moves and not just to the percentage retracement. This is why major bear markets can embrace falls of 38%/39% or of 50%.

## Conclusion

William Gann almost certainly relied on the musical octave to indicate vital support and resistance levels. The generally unknown fact is that each such primary, or outer, octave contains three inner octaves. It is the interaction of these inner octaves with the outer octave that determines the incidence of important boundaries. A bull advance will experience resistance in the region of a 39.3% retracement of the prior bear, and in the region of an 81% retracement of that bear.

In practice, a 39.3% retracement corresponds to a 38.2% retracement. The latter is derived from the golden ratio, 38.2:61.8. This is relevant because a retracement ratio of 38.2% is very important during corrections. The basic rule is that a 38.2% retracement ratio defines the boundary between a correction within an ongoing trend and a reversal in the trend itself. Beyond a 38.2% retracement, the fundamentals that have previously been driving a trend will necessarily reverse or be surmounted by other influences.

Beyond a 38.2% boundary in a falling market, is the 50% boundary. William Gann considered a halving to be very important. We can now see that this is because of the influence of the inner octaves. If a market retraces more than 50% of a previous rise, it is likely to retrace the whole amount.

Finally, each of these ratios may apply to the extent of a move, rather than to the retracement of a previous move. This is why markets can fall by 38%/39% and by around 50%.

# *Appendix III*

## Data For Innovation

### Introduction

The data used in Chapter 14, 'The Pattern of Innovation', has relied on the techniques used by Professor Gerhard Mensch and Professor Jacob van Duijn. Both analysts researched the number of innovations relating to new products over time, and then condensed their findings into sequential time periods. This methodology was not designed to identify the qualitative changes that accrued to one or more innovations, but was designed instead to track phenomena such as clusters of innovations and subsequent discontinuities in the flow of innovations.

The findings of both analysts were similar where they overlap. Professor Mensch's data runs from the late 18th century into the middle of the 20th century, Professor van Duijn's data runs from 1811 to around 1970/71. I have merged the two data series together, and then added information for more recent innovations that can be gleaned from the internet.

### The data

The data consist of two parts: the actual innovation itself and the assimilation of that item into a relevant five-year total. No attempt has been made to assess the effect of an innovation on collective living standards. Moreover, the data after 2009 is only partial.

The charts in Chapter 14 use the innovations shown below. This data has been collected into a sequence of consecutive five-year totals. These totals start in 1795–99 and end in 2005–09.

| Year | Innovation | Year | Innovation |
|------|-----------|------|-----------|
| 1781 | Wattss steam engine | 1856 | Baking powder |
| 1793 | Cotton gin | 1856 | Bessemer steel |
| 1796 | Smallpox vaccination | 1857 | Elevator |
| 1795 | Coke blast furnace | 1859 | Lead battery |
| 1800 | Electricity | 1859 | Oil drilling |
| 1804 | Trevithick steam engine | 1860 | Analine dyes |
| 1808 | Iron anchor chains | 1860 | Combustion engine |
| 1811 | Crucible steel | 1861 | Sodium carbonate |
| 1814 | Gas street lighting | 1863 | Great Metropolitan Rly |
| 1814 | Mechanical printing | 1864 | Siemens-Martin steel |
| 1819 | Lead chamber process | 1866 | Safety matches |
| 1820 | Insulated wiring | 1866 | Atlantic telegraph cable |
| 1820 | Quinine | 1867 | Double armature motor |
| 1820 | Wrought iron rails | 1867 | Dynamite |
| 1822 | Pulled wire | 1869 | Commutator |
| 1824 | Puddling furnace | 1870 | Typewriter |
| 1824 | Portland cement | 1870 | Celluloid |
| 1825 | Stephenson's locomotion | 1870 | Combine harvester |
| 1827 | Pharmaceutical production | 1871 | Margarine |
| 1829 | Coke blast furnace | 1872 | Reinforced concrete |
| 1831 | Potassium chlorate | 1872 | Cylinder armatured motor |
| 1833 | Telegraph | 1873 | Preservatives |
| 1834 | 1st German railroad | 1875 | Gas heating |
| 1835 | Rolled rail | 1875 | Sulphuric acid production |
| 1837 | Electric motor | 1876 | Four stroke engine |
| 1838 | Photography | 1877 | Telephone |
| 1838 | Steamship | 1879 | Light bulb |
| 1839 | Velocipede | 1879 | Electric locomotive |
| 1839 | Electric telegraph | 1879 | Thomas oven |
| 1840 | Vulcanised rubber | 1880 | Water turbine |
| 1844 | Arc lamp | 1880 | Iodoform (antiseptic) |
| 1846 | Electric impulse inductor | 1880 | Chinoline |
| 1846 | Electro measurement | 1880 | Incandescent lamp |
| 1846 | Rotary press | 1880 | Half-tone process |
| 1846 | Anaesthetics | 1882 | Electric heating |
| 1849 | High voltage generator | 1882 | Cable construction |
| 1849 | Steel (puddling process) | 1882 | Cooking fat |
| 1851 | Sewing machine | 1882 | Veronal (barbiturate) |
| 1852 | Plaster cast | 1883 | Phenazone (painkiller) |
| 1855 | Safety match | 1884 | Steam turbine |
| 1855 | Bunsen burner | 1884 | Chloroform |

| Year | Innovation | Year | Innovation |
|------|-----------|------|-----------|
| 1884 | Punched card | 1907 | Electric washing machine |
| 1884 | Cash register | 1909 | Gyro compass |
| 1884 | Fountain pen | 1910 | Long distance telephone |
| 1885 | Transformer | 1910 | High tension insulation |
| 1885 | Chemical fertilizer | 1910 | Airplane |
| 1885 | Cocaine | 1910 | Bakelite |
| 1885 | Bicycle | 1911 | Gyro compass |
| 1886 | Resistance welding | 1913 | Vacuum tube |
| 1886 | Gasoline motor | 1913 | Thermal cracking |
| 1886 | Linotype | 1913 | Domestic refrigeration |
| 1887 | Aluminium | 1913 | Synthetic fertilizer |
| 1887 | Electrolysis | 1914 | Stainless steel |
| 1887 | Aluminium | 1915 | Catalytic cracking (McAfee) |
| 1888 | Meters | 1917 | Cellophane |
| 1888 | Motor car | 1918 | Zip |
| 1888 | Cylindrical record player | 1920 | Acetate rayon |
| 1888 | Portable camera | 1920 | AM radio |
| 1888 | AC generator | 1922 | Insulin |
| 1889 | Record player | 1923 | Hot strip rolling |
| 1889 | Pneumatic tyre | 1924 | Dynamic loudspeaker |
| 1891 | Induction smelting | 1925 | Electric record player |
| 1892 | Oxyacetylene welding | 1926 | Watertight cellophane |
| 1892 | Rayon | 1926 | Tungsten carbide |
| 1894 | Antitoxin | 1930 | Power steering |
| 1894 | Motion picture film | 1930 | Polystyrene |
| 1894 | Motor cycle | 1930 | Rapid freezing |
| 1894 | Monotype | 1930 | Synthetic detergents |
| 1895 | Electric railroad | 1932 | Neoprene |
| 1895 | Refrigeration | 1932 | Synthetic light polarizer |
| 1895 | Diesel engine | 1932 | Gas turbine |
| 1895 | Electric automobile | 1932 | Polyvinylchloride |
| 1896 | X-rays | 1932 | Anti malaria drugs |
| 1897 | Indigo synthesis | 1932 | Synthetic rubber |
| 1898 | Arc welding | 1932 | Crease-resistant fabrics |
| 1898 | Aspirin | 1934 | Diesel locomotive |
| 1898 | Rayon (cuprammonium) | 1934 | Flourescent lighting |
| 1900 | Submarine | 1934 | Radar |
| 1903 | Safety razor | 1935 | Kodachrome |
| 1905 | Viscose rayon | 1935 | Plexiglass |
| 1905 | Vacuum cleaner | 1935 | Rockets |
| 1907 | Purpose built cinema | 1935 | No-knock gasoline |

| Year | Innovation | Year | Innovation |
|------|-----------|------|-----------|
| 1935 | Magnetic tape recorder | 1950 | Radial tyre |
| 1935 | Colour photography | 1951 | Transistor |
| 1935 | Radar | 1951 | Electronic computer |
| 1936 | Helicopter | 1951 | Power steering |
| 1936 | Television | 1952 | Continuous steel casting |
| 1936 | FM radio | 1953 | Cinerama |
| 1937 | Hydraulic clutch | 1953 | Polyethylene (catalyst based) |
| 1937 | Titanium | | |
| 1937 | Catalytic cracking (Sun Oil Co) | 1953 | Oxygen steel making |
| | | 1953 | Colour television |
| 1937 | Electron microscope | 1954 | Gas chromatograph |
| 1938 | Freeze-dried Coffee | 1954 | Remote control |
| 1938 | Rollpoint pen | 1955 | Terylene polyester fibre |
| 1938 | Nylon | 1955 | Controlled machine tools |
| 1938 | Fluorescent lamp | 1956 | Nuclear energy |
| 1938 | Photocopier | 1958 | Fuel cell |
| 1939 | Automatic drive | 1959 | Polyacetates |
| 1939 | Polyethylene | 1959 | Float glass |
| 1941 | Cotton picker (Rust) | 1960 | Polycarbonates |
| 1941 | Jet engine | 1960 | Contraceptive pill |
| 1941 | Penicillin | 1960 | Hovercraft |
| 1942 | Cotton picker (Campbell) | 1961 | Integrated circuit |
| 1942 | Catalytic cracking (Continuous) | 1962 | Communication satellite |
| | | 1964 | Basic prog lang |
| 1942 | DDT | 1964 | IBM 360 computer |
| 1942 | Guided missile | 1964 | Sony VCR |
| 1943 | Silicones | 1965 | Sony Betamax |
| 1943 | Aerosol spray | 1967 | Laser |
| 1943 | High energy accelerators | 1967 | Wankel motor |
| 1944 | Streptomycin | 1968 | Computer mouse |
| 1945 | Sulzer loom | 1969 | Boeing 747 |
| 1946 | Silicones | 1969 | Unix |
| 1946 | Phototype | 1970 | Video cassette recorder |
| 1948 | Continuous steelcasting | 1970 | Dot matrix printer |
| 1948 | Orlon | 1971 | Microprocessor |
| 1948 | Cortisone | 1971 | 8″ floppy drives |
| 1948 | Long-playing record | 1972 | Pocket calculator |
| 1948 | Automatic transmission | 1972 | Gaming console |
| 1948 | Polaroid camera | 1973 | Internet (ARPANET) |
| 1950 | Transistor | 1973 | Floppy disc |
| 1950 | Xerography | 1974 | Bar codes |
| 1950 | Terylene | 1975 | Digital camera |

| Year | Innovation |
|------|-----------|
| 1975 | Cray supercomputer |
| 1976 | VHS |
| 1976 | Ink Jet printer |
| 1977 | Tandy PC |
| 1977 | PC modem |
| 1978 | Atari games console |
| 1978 | Space invaders |
| 1979 | Sony Walkman |
| 1980 | DEC Ethernet |
| 1980 | Pac-Man arcade game |
| 1981 | IBM PC |
| 1981 | Portable laptop |
| 1981 | MS/DOS |
| 1982 | CD player |
| 1983 | Mobile phone |
| 1983 | Camcorder |
| 1983 | Internet (TCP/IP) |
| 1983 | Lotus 1-2-3 |
| 1983 | Microsoft Word |
| 1984 | 3½" floppy disk |
| 1984 | Graphical User Interface |
| 1984 | Apple Mac |
| 1985 | 32-bit computer |
| 1985 | Microsoft windows |
| 1985 | First dot com name |
| 1986 | EMAP |
| 1986 | Intel 386 microprocessor |
| 1986 | First computer virus |
| 1988 | Flat screen TV |
| 1989 | GPS |
| 1989 | Nintendo Gameboy |
| 1989 | Microsoft Office |
| 1990 | 16 megabit chip |
| 1991 | GSM Mobile network |
| 1991 | Unrestricted internet |
| 1991 | Sega Game Gear on handheld |
| 1991 | WWW |

| Year | Innovation |
|------|-----------|
| 1993 | Pentium processor |
| 1993 | Email |
| 1994 | First satellite TV |
| 1994 | Netscape |
| 1994 | Yahoo |
| 1994 | Amazon launched |
| 1995 | Microsoft MSN |
| 1995 | DVD optical disc storage |
| 1995 | Free online advertising |
| 1996 | Internet Explorer 3.0 |
| 1996 | Ebay |
| 1998 | MP3 |
| 1998 | Flash memory |
| 1998 | USB |
| 1998 | Apple iMac |
| 1998 | Nintendo handheld |
| 1999 | Google search engine |
| 1999 | Wi-Fi |
| 1999 | Bluetooth |
| 1999 | Napster |
| 2000 | Hybrid car |
| 2000 | Text messaging |
| 2001 | iPod |
| 2001 | Wikipedia |
| 2002 | Microsoft XBOX |
| 2002 | Camera phones |
| 2003 | Myspace |
| 2005 | Facebook |
| 2005 | Youtube |
| 2006 | Nintendo Wii |
| 2007 | Twitter |
| 2007 | iPhone |
| 2007 | iTouch |
| 2008 | Macbook Air |
| 2008 | Amazon Kindle |
| 2009 | Fitbit activity tracker |
| 2010 | iPad |

## Conclusion

In constructing this list of innovations, I have used the records provided by Professor Gerhard Mensch and Professor Jacob van Duijn. I have then added my own findings to these records in order to cover the developments of more recent years. These additions may not be complete, so other analysts may wish to include the innovations that I have neglected. It may even be necessary to exclude some innovations that I have included. The important criterion, however, is that the data series should, in some sense, be consistent.

My finding is that the data set, for all its limitations, produces a pattern that is almost identical with the pattern that underlies the Life Cycle Hypothesis. It also clearly indicates the fundamental change in the nature of innovation – from collective to personal – as the innovation cycle has evolved.

# *Appendix IV*

## The S-Shaped Learning Cycle

### Introduction

This book suggests that every cycle of transformation and change has a limited time span and is directed by a specific pattern. The existence of a universal, time limited, pattern is the basis of the Life Cycle Hypothesis. Scientific research accepts the idea of a life cycle but relies on a much simpler descriptive pattern.

### Quantitative growth

Most conventional analysis uses a quantitative approach that consists of two parts: an S-shaped 'growth' curve and a bell-shaped 'rate of growth' life cycle. This is shown in Figure AIV-1.

The top part of the diagram shows the relationship between the size of a system and the passage of time. It's 'S' shape (albeit very rightward-leaning) was the basis of the model used by the French sociologist Gabriel Tarde, as long ago as 1890, to demonstrate the non-random spread of imitation.[146] It is almost self-explanatory: the system size starts to increase only slowly, then accelerates, and eventually reaches a maximum. After the maximum size has been reached, some form of 'steady state' will prevail. In principle, the point where no further growth is possible will be determined either by the system's relationship with its environment or by the system's internal framework.

The lower part of the diagram focuses on the **rate** of growth of the S-shaped curve through time. The system comes into being and starts to expand. The measured rate of growth will initially accelerate. Halfway through the process,

---

146  Gabriel Tarde is regarded as the originator of the S-shaped curve. Gabriel Tarde, *Les lois de l'Imitation*, (Félix Alcan, Paris, 1890). Reprinted as *The Laws of Imitation* (Henry Holt, New York, 1903).

however, the rate of growth will reach a maximum. After this, the rate of growth declines. The system itself keeps growing, but it does so at a slower pace. Eventually, when the limit to growth is reached, the rate of growth will drop to zero. At this point, the growth of the system represented by the S-shaped curve is terminated. It follows, therefore, that the symmetrical bell-shaped curve in the lower part of the diagram is the **life cycle** of the process encapsulated in the S-shaped growth curve.

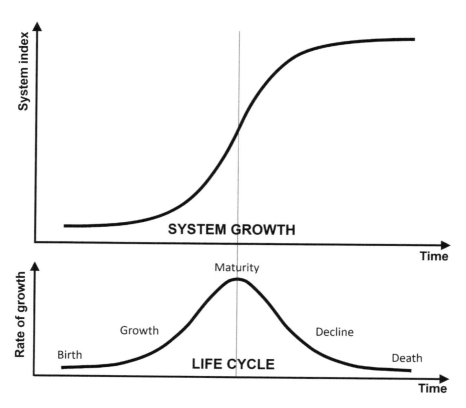

Figure AIV-1: The growth curve and the life cycle

# The Dow Jones Industrial Average

This diagrammatic approach is very powerful, not least because it has certain very specific forecasting applications.[147] Figure AIV-2 highlights the point. It shows the performance of the Dow Jones Industrial Average (DJIA) between 1932 and 1984, measured on a logarithmic scale, together with its five-year rate of change. The peak rate of change in the index occurs just prior to the 1956–57 equity bear market, and is identified by the vertical dashed line. On the basis of the simple life cycle shown in Figure AIV-1, this peak will coincide with the mid-point of the S-shaped growth curve. Figure AIV-2 accordingly includes such a curve.

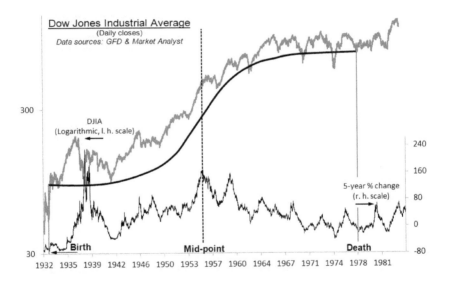

Figure AIV-2: THE DJIA and the S-shaped growth curve

Using seemingly appropriate lows of the rate of change shown in Figure AIV-2, it is possible to estimate that an associated S-shaped curve – and the momentum life cycle – started in 1933 (the 'birth') and ended in 1978 (the

---

147 Gabriel Tarde, *op. cit.* See, for example, Theodore Modis, *An S-Shaped Adventure* (Growth Dynamics, Lugano, Switzerland, 2013). Modis has used the S-shaped curve and its accompanying life cycle for a huge array of valuable purposes. These include such widely diverse objectives as forecasting car safety, tracking the creativity of composers and film producers, and differentiating distinct eras of economic growth from each other.

'death'). These dates are where the momentum lows are about equidistant from the 1954 momentum peak. It is nevertheless obvious that there are alternatives. For example, if the S-shaped curve ended near the bear market low of 1969, the same curve should have started in 1942. This is shown in Figure AIV-3. Alternatively, if the curve ended in 1974, it would have started sometime in 1936. This is shown in Figure AIV-4.

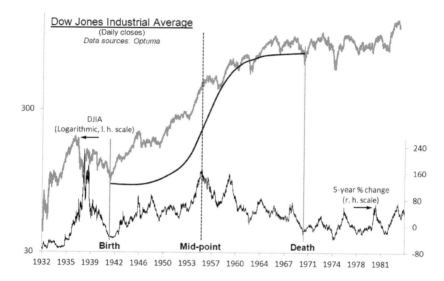

Figure AIV-3: THE DJIA, 1942–69

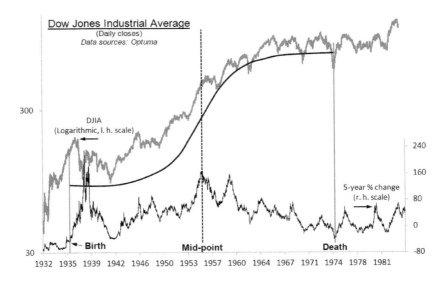

Figure AIV-4: THE DJIA, 1936–74

## Overlapping curves

Each of these possibilities has some validity. With modern computers, it is a relatively simple task to fit a basic S-shaped curve to a graph, and then search for alternatives. In a strongly rising time series that is interspersed with hesitations, it will often be found that a new S-curve starts while an old S-curve is finishing. Consequently, an overall period of growth will consist of a series of overlapping S-shaped curves.[148] For example, in the case of the DJIA, the S-shaped curve that developed between 1933 and 1978 overlapped with the S-shaped curve that evolved between 1966 and 2009. The latter is shown in Figure AIV-5, where it is shown to have reached a momentum peak just prior to the 1987 equity crash. When placed together on the chart in Figure AIV-6, the two curves – which have a very similar duration of between 40 and 45 years – overlap between 1966 and 1978. This was precisely the period when the market was very volatile.

---

148   This has been called 'cascading'. See Theodore Modis, *op. cit.*

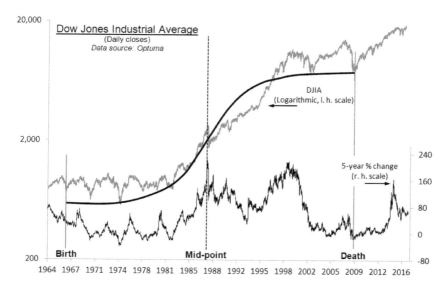

Figure AIV-5: The DJIA, 1965–2009

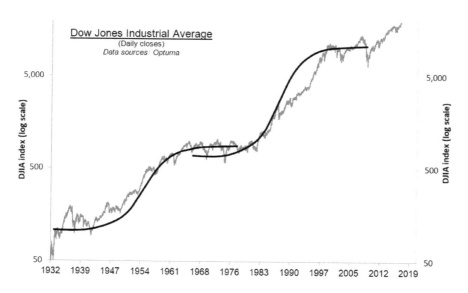

Figure AIV-6: Overlapping S-shaped growth curves

## Projecting into the future

In the foregoing analysis, very little attempt has been made to find a perfect fit between S-shaped growth curves and the behaviour of the DJIA.[149] This means that the conclusions are more indicative than irrefutable. Even so, they are useful. Firstly, the shape of the S-curve means that we can actually infer its presence just from a noticeable sideways movement in a financial market. We may not always be able to calculate precisely where it starts and finishes, but we can expect the curve to project further growth after an obvious mid-cycle momentum peak. All we therefore have to do is recognise that a sideways movement during the so-called 'steady state' at the beginning and end of an S-curve is not necessarily just a flat line. It may have its own internal dynamic. A sideways movement in financial markets is always likely to exhibit some form of oscillation.

Secondly, the combination of an S-shaped growth curve and a rate of growth life cycle means that it is possible to **anticipate** a broad path of development into the future. All that is required is: (a) an estimate for the start of the growth curve and its life cycle; and (b) a properly-identified peak in the rate of growth within the context of an ongoing uptrend. Since the peak rate of growth occurs halfway through the whole process, we can then double the interval between the perceived start and the mid-trend peak (to calculate a potential ending date) and project an S-shaped growth curve into the future (to estimate the extent of the remaining upswing). Despite its simplicity and imprecision, this is a real achievement.

Using this simple methodology, it would have been possible to anticipate future strength in the DJIA at the time of the 1987 equity crash. The crash itself defined the end of an accelerating advance and the start of a period of deteriorating momentum. For many at the time, it felt as if the progress of the previous five years was being reversed. However, the S-shaped curve, which started in the mid-1960s, indicated that the 1987 peak was only halfway through a life cycle that would not end until the first decade of the 21st century.

## Conclusion

When Gabriel Tarde demonstrated the analytical value of the S-shaped growth curve in 1890, he did so in the context not just of quantitative growth but also of learning and evolution. His starting point was that the S-shaped curve reflected the **process** of imitation. Initially, a new product or new idea would have a limited applicability. However, as the attraction of the innovation became

---

149 For a detailed survey of the methodological possibilities, see Theodore Modis, *op. cit.*

obvious, its use would start to spread. New suppliers would enter the market on the basis of creative additions, and/or the original idea would be enhanced and applied more widely. Imitation would not only become more widespread, but the rate of diffusion would accelerate. Eventually, the change would reach a point of maximum penetration – either the market became saturated or the new idea achieved almost universal acceptance. At this point, the process of imitation would level out.

Tarde recognised that the diffusion through an economy of a new product, or the diffusion of an idea through a body of theory, followed an S-shape. Moreover, his model included the idea of the **group mind**, both as the fertile ground for the spread of new ideas and, ultimately, as a constraint on progress. Some of Tarde's concepts were subsequently used by, for example, Gustave Le Bon[150] and Sigmund Freud[151] to progress the theory of crowd behaviour; they subtly informed Ilya Prigogene's[152] theory of self-organising systems, which is now widely used in biology and sociology; and they are directly incorporated into the concept of the S-shaped **learning** curve that is used to explain developments in personal psychology and education.[153] It is an interesting fact that Gabriel Tarde's ideas have themselves followed an S-shape process of evolution – from initial conception, via imitation, to widespread diffusion. The S-curve has become a monument to his genius.

[150] Gustave Le Bon, *La Psychologie des Foules* (Félix Alcan, Paris, 1895). Reprinted as *The Crowd* (Macmillan, New York, 1922).
[151] Sigmund Freud, *Massenpsychologie und Ich-Analyse*, 1921. Reprinted as Group Psychology and the Analysis of the Ego, *Standard Edition*, Vol. XVIII (Hogarth, London, 1981).
[152] Ilya Prigogene and Isabelle Stengers, *Order out of Chaos* (Heinemann, London, 1984).
[153] John O'Neil, *The Paradox of Success* (Tarcher, New York, 1994).

# Index

Milton Keynes UK
Ingram Content Group UK Ltd.
UKHW021948190924
448507UK00006B/153

9 780857 196330